MW01609617

Dream Big

Timeless Principles to Help Realize Your Dream

Annettee Budzban

But Abram said, "O sovereign Lord, what can you give me since I remain childless"
God took him outside and said, "Look up at heavens and count the stars–if indeed you can
count them. So shall your offspring be."
(Genesis chapter 15 verses 2&5 NIV)

God gave Abram a BIG dream!

Contents

Dedication

This book is dedicated to the glorious Father, Son and Holy Spirit (the dream team), who have given me new purpose and meaning to my life and dreams beyond what I could imagine.

Acknowledgements

$\mathcal{I}$ thank all the Christian authors and teachers that have trans- formed my thinking through their powerful words and messages. A special thanks to Jenny Vlahos and Vicki den exter Blockland for their contribution and input in editing. I thank my favorite writing companion, Nancy Gibbs, who over the years has spent countless hours talking on the phone sharing writing and speaking experiences with me.

To my supportive friend of 37 years, Babe Stanley who was my nurse co-entrepreneur in teaching childbirth classes; and has hung in there with me through life's journey of ups and downs.

To my three sons, Jimbo, Tim and Adam, my stepdaughter Molly and her husband, Mike. To my grandchildren Timmy, Katelynn, Crystall, Vic, Jake, Brock and Violet all whom I love beyond words, and have played a part in molding and shaping my life role as grandmother.

To my husband Jeffrey, alias, "Buzz" who experienced and weathered his share of hardships alongside of mine and beautified my writing with his creative cover designs.

Above all, I acknowledge our everlasting Lord, WHO has filled me with His Spirit, and given me the Bible-the GREATEST story ever told.

A few others who have blessed my BIG Dream with their love, prayers and support:

My BIG sister Lea Dussault Weber who has clothed me with great hand-me-downs that have filled my closet and wise words that have warmed my soul.

My special Friends:

Sue Anderson Helmke

Bernice Zegan Sharon Giranda Jan Arnold

Diane Weber Bonnie Klowas Julie Sagel (my sweet niece)

Rosa Prosen Edie Wilt Karen Bethel

My lady friends from Stonecroft Women's Connection Lake County, Il., Vonnie, Linda and Lynn.

Introduction

"The end of a matter is better than its beginning..."

(ECCLESIASTES 7:8 NIV)

Do you dare to dream? I've always enjoyed dreaming. When I was a young girl I used to enjoy reading adventure books. I, oftentimes, read the ending first because I believed in *happily ever after*. Then I would go back and read how the story began and fill in the life changing details. Little did I realize that is how our dreams develop. First we visualize in our minds the end of our dream; then in reality we take the detailed steps to fulfill it.

"No eye has seen, no ear has heard, no mind has conceived what God has prepared for those who love him" (1 Corinthians 2:9 NIV).

Dreams take many forms. We have daydreams, night dreams and sometimes elusive, shattered or broken dreams. Oftentimes, we have untapped talents or dormant dreams, information that lay deep in our hearts that goes unnoticed or untouched. We may possess latent dreams and shrug our shoulders and think it's too late or impossible to fulfill them. I found out it's the impossible dreams that God is looking to fulfill.

Dreams and Detours

At a recent speaking engagement the hostess called me a, *"Dream Liver"*- I kind-of liked that title. However, several years ago I didn't think that was possible. I was in the prime of my career as a nurse manager for eighteen years, along with my side business of sixteen years, as a childbirth educator. I had some career aspirations stirring in my soul. Due to my Christian faith I enjoyed praying for healing with my patients. That gave me a desire to become a Congregational Health Nurse. A Congregational Health Nurse or Parish Nurse, is a nurse employed by a hospital and placed in a church congregation or parish to instruct on issues that promote physical, emotional, and spiritual health and well-being. The position includes setting up health screenings such as monthly blood pressure checks. The nurse also teaches classes on Smoking Cessation, Weight Loss or other health issues. Other duties include sick visitation, and administering the spiritual practices of prayer for the sick and the offering of communion. I applied for a position in that specialty 3 times, but nothing materialized. So, I laid my desire aside and figured due to my family responsibilities it wasn't the right time for making a job change to pursue that dream.

I was also a single divorced mother for ten years, with some shattered romantic dreams, but working two jobs and raising three rambunctious sons, didn't leave much time for dating or finding the man my heart desired.

Then one day while I was home doing weekly household chores, I was startled by a knock on the door. I swung the door open expecting to see one of my son's friends on the other side. Instead it was an old acquaintance I had met some years before in a church drama group.

God brought a new man into my life and a whirlwind romance that offered me the dream of a new beginning at life, love and marriage, and the daughter I desired.

We had a fairytale, candlelight wedding ceremony and reception on the night of Valentine's Day at the church where we met.

Around midnight, before departing the reception for our honeymoon, we sat on a church pew in the dim lit Sanctuary and discussed our dreams for an adventure filled future. But our dreams didn't turn out as we planned. Let me take you back a few years...

— ⌣ —

In Search of *Dreams*

Unexpected dreams had taken place and future ones were under way as Jeff and I embarked on our new life together. As newlyweds, we often shared quiet moments and pillow talk. In these personal times we'd discuss our desire for vacations and fun with our family, and laughed how we might be as we grew old together. We also talked about secret career goals tucked deep within our hearts.

With my new husband, empty nest, and career goals intact, I was determined to make my dreams come true. While working my current job, I searched the nursing want ads for Congregational Health Nurse positions. I attended conferences and started taking College classes to further my degree and increase my chances of landing my dream job. I figured I was on the right path and that it was only a matter of time ... However in the midst of my new life goals and plans, an illness that had entered my life just two years before, started coming back with a vengeance. Suddenly these newlyweds' lives were turned upside-down.

Just before I dated Jeff I was diagnosed with Environmental Illness. One day, while working at the clinic I started breaking out in rashes and itching. Visual disturbances erupted and I saw squiggly lines and light flashes in my field of vision. On occasion I would feel cold, anxious, fatigued and my muscles were stiff and achy. I felt foggy headed and had difficulty concentrating.

My doctor tried me on every allergy medication there was on the market, but nothing worked. Then while on the medications I started feeling weak, shaky, and faint. Digesting food after meals caused lethargy, stiff muscles, pain, rashes, itching, blisters and swelling on my inner cheeks and tongue. Cold shivers went up and down my spine and all over my body. The bottom of my feet felt like hot burning coals and at times I had sharp stabbing pains in my body that felt like I was being stung by bees.

When my internist couldn't figure out what to do I searched out an environmental allergist. He suggested a few things I hadn't tried such as diet changes and a mild anti- fungal medication. Allergy testing was impossible when I reacted to the chemical Phenol or Glycerin base in the solutions. Through blood tests it was discovered that I had developed sensitivities to many foods, medications and environment molds and chemicals. I was also diagnosed with a troubling digestive disorder that caused many of these problems. Besides all of this this my liver wasn't detoxing like it should and the buildup of toxins was creating these troubling symptoms. It was discovered my stiffness and achiness in my muscles and internal organs turned out to be Fibromyalgia. I felt like I was falling apart.

I found some temporary relief from a few of the symptoms by following dietary changes, avoidance of moldy places and small doses of a mild antifungal medication, I was able to handle. I thought the worst of this distressing ailment was behind me.

One day, while riding in the car I noticed I was getting sleepy and could hardly stay awake. My breathing was labored and difficult. The aggravating sensations of cold, numbness and pain traveled through my body all the way to my fingertips. The stabbing, burning pain in my feet was so bad I couldn't walk on them. Not to mention the fear, anguish and emotional frustration I felt. With my beloved new husband at my side, we searched for answers and help to these incapacitating sensitivities. We traveled all over northern, IL. to several different specialists; homeopathic physicians, chiropractors, and environmental allergists were among the list. Some offered insight to the problem, but due to the fact I was sensitive to many of the medications and supplements I needed to take it was difficult to treat. The menu selection for my daily meals was dwindling before me as I was down to only a few foods I could eat without serious reactions. Taking any medications or supplements only led to more troubling reactions and health problems.

As time passed the burning pain in my feet became unbearable. I was hospitalized for two weeks to some take tests. During my hospitalization I responded to a treatment that provided me some relief from the foot pain through a holistic doctor. However, not long after my release from the hospital, riding in the car became a big issue for me. Car exhausts from the traffic caused my symptoms to erupt. I couldn't ride in the car without breathing difficulties and other disturbing symptoms. Going outside was challenging in hot or cold weather. Anyone with asthma can relate.

Eventually many other symptoms worsened; our hopes diminished and, due to medical expenses, our savings dwindled down to nothing. In a short period of time our happily ever after turned into a nightmare as I became housebound and unable to go outside of our home. Can you imagine what it's like not to be able to go out of your home? Within the same month I became housebound, my oldest sister died and a week to the day later my father passed away. I wondered, *was I next?*

In a blink of the eye I lost my health, career, beloved family members and my weekly paycheck. With all these changes I felt bewildered. On top it, I was adjusting to a new home in a new neighborhood and I was a recent empty-nester. Then one day the phone rang. It was my best friend, Sue. I'd known her since we were in fifth grade. She offered a lot of comfort and solace to me in my time of need, however, this call contained news that was anything but comforting when she informed me her husband had taken a new job in another state and they would be moving in six weeks!

With that news I fell into despair. I started feeling hopeless, isolated and afraid. One day while sitting in a cozy corner of my bedroom, my favorite spot for prayer, I thought how I attended Sunday school as a young girl. I was fascinated by the true Bible stories of miracles Jesus performed by faith. I felt like a woman that was mentioned in one of them. She had a health issue too. I could identify with her because she had been to many physicians unable to treat her...it says she spent all her money but only grew worse, just like I had. As I read the Bible passage, I thought, *I can identify with her.* To find her answer she turned to faith in Jesus and was healed (this story is found in the Bible book of Mark chapter 25, verse 34.) Because I could compare my story with hers, I found solace in pondering this passage. Besides this story, I knew Jesus was my only answer. I recalled how He gave me eternal life. As a child I realized I was a sinner and the payment for that sin was eternal separation for God. The Bible says, "For the wages of sin is death, but the free gift of God is eternal life through Jesus Christ our Lord" (Romans 6:23 NIV). I learned that Jesus Christ is the Son of God Who came to earth to die on the cross in place of our sins. Three days after His death, God raised Him back to life. Those who believe in Jesus can be reconciled back to God, saved from the penalty of eternal death in Hell and have a relationship with Him and talk with Him. We experience this reality simply through believing.

"For it is by grace you have been saved through faith-and this not from yourselves, it is the gift of God-not by works, so that no one can boast" (Ephesians 2:8 NIV).

I reminisced about that day I had invited Jesus to forgive my sins. I knew Jesus was a living presence in my life and had done many miraculous things over the years in answer to my prayers...but now I faced some of the most difficult days I'd ever faced. I wondered, "What would He do for me now? Would Jesus heal me? How long would I have to wait?"

A Dream Discovered

A recent acquaintance of mine explained that she got up early each morning and prayed. She read her Bible and expected God to speak to her personally through His Word. I noticed a passage in the Bible that says, "Very early while it was dark, Jesus got up, and went off to a solitary place, where he prayed" (Mark 1:35).

After that, each morning before the sun starting beaming through the blinds, I got out of bed and stumbled down the dark hallway to the couch in our living room. Nestling into my comfy, corner spot on the sofa I cleared my mind and opened my Bible as I sat and spent time with God. Sometimes I read Bible verses hoping something enlightening would jump off the page; other times, I sat quietly with my eyes closed waiting for some insight or idea to come to mind.

Morning after morning, month by month I repeated my ritual of spending time with God.

One morning while nestled in my secret place of communion with God, I held my eyes closed and paused from my requests to listen. I heard a soft gentle voice from within whisper, *"Write."*

"Lord, I don't know how to write...I am a nurse not a writer." I replied to this voice.

But, as I carefully listened, the thought came back more definitive this time, *"Write!"*

To search into this matter a little further, I responded with a request, *"God, if this is you and you want me to write, send me a typewriter at no cost to me."*

About a month later, the phone rang. It was my sister. *"I just bought a new computer and wondered if you would like my Word Processor,"* she asked.

I was stunned and amazed when I realized my request had been granted! I accepted her generous offer and started pondering what it was I would write.

I had been doing tremendous amounts of Bible study and God had been giving me new insights and understanding about the practical spiritual principles of life.

I was also beginning to realize we were all created by God with a specific purpose. I used to think that my vocational desires and other dreams were my idea and God fulfilled them in his plan and time, however, I realized many times God places those desires in our hearts and we need to pray them through and carry them out. "Delight yourself also in the Lord, and He will give you the desires and secret petitions of your heart" (Psalm 37:4).

God was showing me a new direction and purpose for *my* life. As God started showing me I was constructed in a certain way, (You knit me together in my mother's womb Psalm 139:3 AMP) I wanted to know more about his plans and purpose for me. I discovered reading books on purpose and studying Scripture passages on God's purposes helpful.

One of many passages that touched me was this one: "We have different gifts, according to the grace given us. If a man's gift is prophesying, let him use it in proportion to his faith. If it is serving, let him serve; if it is teaching, let him teach; if it is encouraging, let him encourage; if it is contributing to the needs of others, let him give generously; if it is leadership, let him govern diligently; if it is mercy, let him do it cheerfully"(Romans 12:6-8 NIV).

Jeff was great about picking up the slack of errands and shopping. One day after returning home from a typical shopping trip he handed me a paper sack. I reached into the bag and pulled out a package of beautiful, celery green stationary, with angels dressed in white cascading down the side of the paper. I reached my hand inside the bag once more and pulled out a pack of matching envelopes. I started writing devotions on my angel stationary and sending them to my friends. The response was overwhelming.

Many of my friends replied back, *"This is great. I got just the right message on the right day! I enjoy receiving those special 'Angelopes' in my mailbox!"*

They even requested I send them to their friends; a few of them bought me more envelopes and stationary so I'd have them on hand. I was enjoying my new purpose in devotional/inspirational writing. I had been feeling hopeless, depressed and insolated now God gave me a new purpose and a reason to get out of bed each morning.

Over time, I felt I was being led by the Lord to do something more with my writing. During my Bible study time I enjoyed reading the Scriptures as if God was speaking directly to me. I realized that some-times we can get general information to guide our lives, other times God speaks to us specifically through a passage.

One particular day, while thumbing through the pages of my Bible, my emotions were stirred when I read the words, *"Go publish."* After that it seemed almost every time I picked up my Bible I came across Scriptures containing the word publish. It was becoming evident as to what my next step was regarding my devotional articles.

For a few weeks I pondered over my new direction. I asked a friend who knew someone that was connected with a publisher if she could find out how I would go about getting something published. Within a short time she gave me a note from him with list of things to point me in that direction. With nothing else to do I started my journey of making sub-missions to magazines and others places. You could imagine my elation when I received my first acceptance letter for an article. As time went on I was published in places such as *Guideposts Angels on Earth, Guideposts books, Cup of Comfort devotionals, New York Times Best Seller Chicken Soup for the Recovering Soul* and *Chicken Soup for the Soul: Inspiration for Nurses* and many other secular and Christian publications. A few nursing publications were publishing my submissions as well. Eventually my first book, *Life Changing Inspirations* was birthed. It was a collection of the inspirational devotions I had been writing for my friends. I realized as I learned to listen to God in the midst of my adversity I discovered a hidden talent and 'bloomed where I was planted.' This old cliché was starting to make sense.

As I continued my journey of writing and publishing, one day, Jeff came in from a shopping trip and placed several bags of groceries on the table. I noticed a newspaper tucked in between the brown, paper shopping bags. I picked it up and unfolded it to the front page and read the name of the newspaper, Daily Herald.

"Is this a new paper in Lake County? I never heard of it before." I immediately inquired of Jeff.

"No," was Jeff's reply. *"It's been around for a long time. I used to deliver it when I had my paper route several years ago."*

Instinctively I opened it up to the section listing the names and numbers of each editor. I went to the phone, dialed the number and asked to speak with the editor. I quickly told them my story; that I was a nurse and became housebound with an illness and felt a call to write. I explained about my writing ministry and many of the places I had been published. Within two months the editor called me and conducted a phone interview. I remember how amazed I was as I read the headlines of that article: "Illness Inspires Creation of Writing Ministry." After my story appeared I contacted the editor about doing a weekly column. At his request, I submitted samples of my Inspirational writings for him to read. Seven weeks later my column, "Inspirations" appeared in the paper.

One day while flipping through my Bible, I came across this Scripture verse, "Write down the revelation... that a herald may run with it" (Habakkuk 2:2 NIV). I felt it was a personal message to me. At that moment I realized I was writing God's vision in a herald, (the name of the paper), to thousands of people so they could live with purpose and powerful principles to fulfill their God-given dreams.

In the midst of my new passion to help others through writing I was still sick and hurting. There were days I was fatigued and depressed and didn't feel like doing anything. The mental and physical anguish felt tortuous. However, I still prayed daily asking God for my healing. I knew He was my only hope.

One day during my Bible study time, I was reading in the book of Judges how Gideon had asked God to give him a sign if he was going to defeat his enemies in battle. I thought, *"That's what I need; a sign from God."*

So I asked, *"God give me a sign if I am really going to be healed."*

I thought for a moment what I might want it to be. I reasoned with myself it would have to be something unusual; like a deer coming into my back yard. I live in a residential area where it was highly unlikely to spot any deer. Even my next-door-neighbor who had lived here for twenty years said she'd never seen a deer roaming around any of the yards in this neighborhood. So that's what I asked for.

Each day after that prayer I eagerly looked for my dear. I would gaze out the kitchen window anticipating and dreaming of where from the wooded area behind my house the brown, four-legged creature might come from.

One warm, sunny summer afternoon, Jeff decided to dismiss his usual Sunday routine of mowing the back lawn. Instead, he decided to go into our bedroom and watch the NASCAR race. This was quite unusual because Jeff enjoyed keeping our lawn plush green and meticulously manicured. I was in the living room visiting with my niece. About mid race Jeff got up from the bed and went into the kitchen for something. He said he wasn't even quite sure what he wanted.

Glancing out the window he paused and said, *"Annettee, Julie...quick... come here! But be real quiet... There's a deer in our back yard!"*

You can imagine how my heart leapt in my chest. In one unexpected moment my prayer had been answered. I wasn't sure whether to laugh or cry. I felt riveted to the floor, yet, I couldn't get to the window fast enough to see my deer!

Leaning over the kitchen sink I looked out the window into the back yard. When I caught sight of the deer my gaze locked in place, while I embraced the magnificent moment. Every detail stood out from the shiny, brown coat to the furry, white tail.

I watched intently while my visitor nibbled from my birdfeeder enjoying a mid-day snack. Seed fell to the ground as the feeder swayed back and forth from the shepherd's hook. As the deer lingered there munching for quite some time, Jeff ran and grabbed the video camera to capture the special moment on video tape. The following week, I shared the video with my pastor. A few weeks later, he showed the tape to our church congregation. After that, from-time-to time when my friends from church would spot a deer they would call me and say, "*I saw a deer today!*" It was their way of acknowledging my healing was on the way. Over the next few years I watched that tape time and again.

For my birthday Jeff bought me a concrete statue of a deer and placed it in our yard in the same spot my deer appeared. Each time I looked out the kitchen window it served as a reminder of God's precious promise to me. I even named my deer, Promise!

I pondered that I had been given my promise. But like someone waiting to be released from prison, (I often thought of the story of Joseph who was unjustly imprisoned. Genesis 37-50), I didn't know when I'd be let out of my personal one. I only knew it would happen in God's time.

Day-after day, month after month, year after year, I waited for the fulfillment. There were times tears stained my pillow, as I sobbed myself to sleep. There were days I would pour my heart into writing in my prayer journal to ease the hurt and pain. "*God, I need your help. Please heal my body so I can go outside again and help others and enjoy my family and friends.*" There were other times I sat in my rocking chair and swayed and prayed. I missed special occasions with my children. Weddings, births of grandchildren and family gatherings were some of those special times I longed to be a part of. To avoid getting too down I kept up with my weekly column and other submissions. I was gaining great strides in my writing ministry.

In the meantime, God was still weaving the patchwork of my dreams. With my new passion for writing I had set aside the fact that I was a nurse. I kept my nursing license up-to-date, (I paid to dear a price to let go of that), but I detached myself from that aspect of my life. Occasionally I would write an article on the connection between mind, body and Spirit health, but I hadn't really considered my dream to become a congregational nurse anymore. Yet, each month my free copy of

Nursing Spectrum magazine still appeared in my mailbox. I never bothered to open a page; I just threw it in the trashcan. I called the office and cancelled my subscription; but it still appeared in my mailbox!

One day after receiving the magazine, I was about to loosen my grip and drop it in the garbage can when I suddenly stopped, and opened it. The page which opened up read: "Entrepreneurial Fire!" I quickly scanned the page. It explained how nurses make great writers, speakers and life coaches. That caught my attention. As the article resonated with my soul I felt led to speak, write and consider life coaching. In one short article I discovered two more pieces to my purpose: Speaking and Life Coaching. I didn't know how they would come about, but I knew they were God- given gifts that stirred the passion within me to purse them.

Since I wasn't sure what a life coach was, after reading the article, I turned detective and did some investigating. Articles on life coaching miraculously appeared on my Internet page without searching for them; somehow they showed up in my e-mails or magazines I was reading. I realized life coaching was another way to help people achieve their life goals. In nursing school I was taught how to establish goals and strategies for each of my patients. I knew this was the perfect vehicle for helping people achieve health goals. As a nurse I helped multiple patients develop and achieve their health goals this way. Now I realized this process was a practice I could extend to Spiritual, career or personal development goals as well!

Since I couldn't go out and speak, God gave me creative ways to accomplish His plan. I started doing Teleseminars. Callers dialed in a special number I gave them through a phone service I signed up with. This connected us in a conference call with participants from across the nation. With all my new talents surfacing I named my ministry, "Be Inspired!" because, I was out to inspire others to open their hearts to the knowledge, love and gifts of Jesus Christ.

One day while speaking to an editor about my columns she inspired me with her words, *"Annettee, you're no longer a childbirth educator; but instructing others to birth their God-given dreams and visions."* This comment was a confirmation to words I'd already heard whispered to my heart at an earlier time.

— ᵔ —

Restoring the Years and Dreams

The clock was ticking away. Days turned into weeks, weeks turned into months and years turned into eight or nine since I became housebound. Sometimes, the promise seemed like a faded memory or an elusive dream I was unable to capture. And just when I thought the worst was behind me more adversity hit. My symptoms kept growing worse. My family started falling apart. One of my children was diagnosed with a serious illness. Another lost his business and his marriage dissolved. The other one got divorced and suffered an illness and was unable to work for a period of time; he eventually lost his home, car and belongings to foreclosure. I was emotionally shaken that my son's lives were falling apart and I couldn't help them. The mother and nurse in me longed to tend to their emotional and physical needs when they were ill and aid their finances to help relieve their burden. I spent time with them on the phone counseling and encouraging them, whenever I could.

Then I noticed my beloved husband was showing signs of depression. He was crabby, short tempered and emotionally distant. As I watched his behavior, I realized the dream for my healing was fading for him.

Praying about the situation, I noticed a basket in the corner of the living room with some books in it. The title of one caught my attention, "1001 Ways to Be Romantic"; I remembered I bought that book when Jeff and I were newlyweds, as I had wanted to find ways to keep the romantic passion alive between the two of us. As I stared at the cover; I realized we were in need of rekindling the romance in our lives. Somewhere while we waited for my healing to manifest, we fell into the mundane routine of taking care of business.

Although I wasn't feeling my best, I reached outside of myself. I wrote love notes on Post-It's and placed them around the house. I had a friend pick up a fragrant red rose from the corner florist and graced his pillow with one. I placed an old card he had given me along side of the rose and posted a new sentiment such as, "Ditto" on the card and signed it.

One day, I noticed a woman walking down our street. The spring in her step and the bounce in her hair caught my attention. In the past I always enjoyed looking good. I rarely went out without applying make-up and dressing in an outfit that matched or accented my best features. I wasn't out to impress, but always felt that looking good is part of a person's self-esteem. It shows we care about ourselves.

I stared at an old photo on top of the Television. I longed to look like that again. I glanced down at my ragged and torn house dress and the lifeless strands of dull graying hair; unlike my lustrous brunette strands in the picture. Thinking about the healthy glow on my face in that photo, a wee-little whisper crept up from inside of me, *"There's minerals make-up on the market now-a-days...maybe you could use some of that without reacting."*

I rushed to my computer and looked for sites with the brand of make-up I used to wear. I found some minerals cosmetics in their line. I ordered some right away.

I was excited the day my package arrived in the mail; I tore it open like a child on Christmas morning. I looked over my order, grabbed some blush, ran to the mirror and applied it to my pale, white complexion. When I looked at myself in the mirror I felt better. I noticed how a little color on my cheeks livened up my face. I was able to wear some make-up-no rashes, eye watering, no severe reactions! Sometimes, I had to change the brand or try something different because of the reactions. But Like a dedicated soldier I stayed the course and put some effort into fixing my make-up and hair.

One day, tired of my old worn-out attire, I decided to rifle through my closet to see what was available. I hadn't really shopped in years. I pulled out a blue sparkling blue top my sister had given me just a few months before. I put it on. How dazzling I looked with a little sparkle.

I started listening to old songs on the radio. I noticed as I was feeling alive again, my faith was rising.

My attitude toward my illness improved, and my outlook on life became more positive. I focused on healing Scriptures such as, "For I will restore health to you, and I will heal your wounds, says the Lord" (Jeremiah 30:17). This helped me get rid of thoughts about how bad I physically felt. A friend of mine informed me about a nutritional bio-chemist that had some new insights on some supplements for me to try. It took me six months to take one capsule, but I was elated to be able to accomplish this.

As I was willing to make changes, I felt God helping me make prog-ress and improve my life.

Then in my prayer time a message came, "Go back to church." I was astonished by the message and replied, "Lord, how can I do that?"

By faith, I set a date for the next two weeks. It was the day before my 53rd birthday. *"What a great birthday gift,"* I thought. But as the days went by I fought double mindedness and uncertainty. I pondered this verse of Scripture, "Believe and do not doubt" (James 1:6 NIV). I needed to stay in faith and fight the doubt so I could succeed. Part of me was excited at the thought of getting out into the world again. Yet, another part of me felt anxious and afraid of encountering the same disappointments from past attempts. I held on to the promise for my healing. In my prayer time I reminded God of the sign of that deer, in order to keep my focus straight.

I strengthened my faith as I searched through my closet for some-thing special to wear. Over the years I had given a lot of my clothing away. To me giving is an important aspect of spiritual maturity that prevents us from becoming greedy and brings a blessing back to us.

Shuffling the hangers, I kept in mind that I felt most comfortable in clothing that was primarily 100% cotton. Since it had been years since I had the pleasure of dressing up to go anywhere, I decided to be a little playful. I came across a black dress with mauve colored roses. It had a small jacket that matched and tied into a sweet bow in the front. It was cute, casual and fit comfortably. It was one of my favorites from the past. It was the perfect dress for my coming out party and early summer attire. *But what would I wear on my feet?* I thought.

I usually wore slippers around the house. They were soft and comfy for my feet that were stiff and achy from the Fibromyalgia in my muscles. Besides my clothes, I had also given away most of my shoes. I pulled out a plastic shoe bin from the bottom of my closet. Sorting through the few pairs left, I came across a pair of sandals my sister gave to me. They were held on by a few thin straps. Anything too constrictive made my feet stiff and achy. I tried on the sandals. They fit well and still afforded me the freedom from being confining for the condition my feet were in.

With my plans in motion, I prayed diligently as I awaited Sunday's arrival. I kept my faith strong as I believed to move forward toward my healing.

It was a beautiful sunny, summer day in the beginning of June. As I stepped outside the door I heard birds chirping. I got into the car and nestled in my bucket seat. Jeff had to remind me to put my seat belt on. I reached for the shoulder harness, pulled it across my chest, and snapped the buckle in place. Funny, how what was once such a routine part of my life now felt awkward. After the seatbelt clicked in place, Jeff placed the car in gear and we were off.

As I rode through the neighborhood I tried to get my mind off of myself by looking at the colorful blooms in each neighbor's yard.

A few blocks away, I started feeling some of the old symptoms coming back. But I spoke healing Scriptures to myself such as: "By His wounds you have been healed," (1 Peter 2:24).

As we rode down the streets I felt a sense of awe and amazement that I was actually out of my house. I gazed at some of the old stores we frequented. Instead of focusing on my symptoms I concentrated on the aspect of how freeing it was to go out again.

As I noticed the church building, my stomach filled with butterflies. We pulled into the lot and parked close to the door. My heart started racing, as I exited the car and headed for the double doors to enter the church.

At the entrance I was greeted by a petite, attractive lady with a warm and welcoming smile. She introduced herself and handed me a bulletin and I proceeded toward the sanctuary. I walked only a few feet to the sanctuary door. I spotted an empty pew in the back of the church. I sat at the end. I didn't want to be near anyone with strong perfumes or deodorants since these were things that triggered symptoms in the past.

Sitting there for a few moments I noticed I was starting to have a little difficulty. I decided not to panic. I was distracted when the worship started. I was overwhelmed by the beautiful music as I listened to the electric piano, drums, guitars and singers. Tears welled up in my eyes and I sat riveted in my pew. My voice quivered with emotion as I sang along in worship. I couldn't believe I was in church again. I embraced every moment.

During the ride home I turned some old familiar tunes on the car radio and sang along as we drove down the streets to our home.

Arriving home I sat in my chair and took a deep breath. I looked at the clock and thought to myself, "I've been out of my house over an hour, for the first time in about eight years!"

The rest of the day I was filled with joy. I wanted to do this again.

Persevering in prayer, the thought came to me to start walking in my driveway each day. I didn't waste any time. The next day I went out for five minutes. After that, each day when I got up I studied my Bible, prayed, ate breakfast and then took my morning walk! I had a new routine! Throughout the weeks ahead I worked my way up to being out for 20-30 minutes at a time. I was amazed how well I was handling being outside again. With my new determination, I found reasons to go outside...I made it a habit to go out and get the mail each day. I would also have Jeff drive me to our local beach so I could adjust to car rides. It was good for me, and stirred the romantic fires in our hearts. I was determined the devil was never going to keep me housebound with these symptoms anymore. I was in awe as I experienced the miraculous taking place in my life.

It was amazing to get out and see all the new sights and expanding communities. Going to a mega store was an overwhelming and fascinating experience. I'd smile when I'd come home from an outing and discover a message on my answering machine from one of my friends. They usually said something like this... "I tried to contact you, but I guess you're not home...that's a good thing!"

I'd seen God restoring the years I'd lost---only it was better than before!

A special dream came true when I was able to attend my oldest grandson's graduation---a family occasion! It had been a desire of his. He would often say, *"Grandma, I wish you could make it to my graduation."* With the Lord's help I did!

Six months after going out of my house I started getting invitations for speaking. I've spoken to grief groups, seniors, MOPS, and women's groups, the medical society, job seekers and was the key note speaker for the nation-wide volunteer's conference for Cancer Treatment Centers of America. But the greatest of all, was the conference held at Concordia University for Congregational Health Nurses- I wanted to be one... I never dreamt of speaking there and teaching them!

I'm still building my dreams. I still battle serious health challenges, but in the meantime I believe for the promise for my total recovery to manifest.

Through all the detours of my life, God has been there meeting my need. If I hadn't opened my heart to Him I wouldn't have been able to find purpose and meaning in those years of being housebound. I found God's dreams for us are greater than the ones we have for ourselves. I realized that God fulfilled my dream to become a congregational health nurse, only it was on a larger scale and greater than I imagined! I'm not just teaching one congregation like I desired, instead the world is my congregation, as I speak, teach and write all over! To confirm this, I was recently approached to have one of my articles used in a book for students in another country.

God has BIG DREAMS planted inside each of us just waiting to be fulfilled. A dream specifically designed for each one. In my wildest dreams I never would have imagined God would call me to write. It's not as if I grew up with a desire to become an author (when my friend asked me to take a creative writing class, I declined), or a professional speaker- I hated speech class! I was so quiet and shy most people thought I was an extreme introvert or stuck up! Instead I was an extrovert who needed some stretching to reach my potential.

Through my housebound experience, I found out it's in our painful and adverse places that we can discover who God planned us to be. "For

I know the plans I have for you," declares the Lord, "Plans to prosper you and not to harm you, plans to give you hope and a future" (Jeremiah 29:11 NIV). When we seek God through prayer, study our Bible and remain open-minded to the Scripture verses with new dreams and possibilities they hold, we find more about us than what we could imagine.

Our God-given dreams take time, wisdom and the leading and the strength of God's Holy Spirit to help us achieve each step. He can use our adversity for His good if we cooperate with Him. He can do greater things far above what we imagine can happen! What better way to live than with the anticipation that God has a dream for us and delights in watching us discover it. We serve a BIG God that is able to do "superabundantly, far over *and* above and all that we [dare] ask or think [infinitely beyond our highest prayers, desires, thoughts, hopes, or dreams] (Ephesians 3:20).

Have you taken the time to dream lately? Have you ever asked yourself what does God desire for my life? What specific plans does He have in mind for me? What am I supposed to become? I'd like to help you with that within the following chapters. There were ancient Scriptural principles that the Lord taught me to help make my dreams become realities... Precious friends, I want to share them with you. Would you dare to dream?

— ~

Dreams and Desire

Do you have a dream for the future? Do you know what you're dreaming for? Have you ever pondered what lies ahead for the God-given plan in your life?

At a speaking event a woman approached me and said she doesn't think she dreams.

"Do you pray?" I asked her.

"Yes," she replied.

Those things you are requesting in your prayers are what you're dreaming for.

I don't know what you're dreaming about. Maybe you have relationship issues that you desire to see resolved. Most of us have one kind of issue or another.

Maybe you'd like to build a business. My ministry is my business. I have aspirations for my children and grandchildren I would like to see fulfilled, as many of you have. Perhaps you'd like to own your own home or be debt free or get free from an addiction...our list of desires can seem endless.

Whatever your desire is it's your dream. I'll share a few of my favorite Scriptures about dreams. They prove that it is God's plan that we dream big! The Bible is a book of dreams. It contains true stories of the dreams God planted in men and women to be used to fulfill His great dream for mankind, to bring us a Savior. Now, God wants to use you in the great scheme of things!

"He who reveals secrets was making known to you
what shall come to pass"

(DANIEL 2:29 LIVING BIBLE).

"...your old men dream dreams your young men shall see visions"

(JOEL 2:28 AND ACTS 2:19).

The principles in this book are inspirational and informative. I learned them firsthand by spending time with God. They are intertwined with experiences, insights and powerful Scripture verses meant to instruct and inspire you to discover, pursue, embrace and act on your special, divinely guided dreams and heart's desire. You will often hear me refer to them as dream steps, because they are the stepping stones to our dreams. Yet they are powerful principles not to be taken lightly. There is no particular order to them. But utilized they can help make your dreams come true.

If your dreams and aspirations have not become a reality yet, allow these time-tested principles to help you step out into the reality of your dream.

1

Develop a Relationship with the Dream Giver - It's the Relationship to Your Dream

"Call to Me, I will answer you, and show you great and mighty things, you do not know."

~JEREMIAH 33:3

You can't dream big without first pursuing a relationship with the dream giver. "For God so loved the world that he gave his one and only Son, that whoever believes in him shall not perish but have eternal life" (John 3:16 NIV).

Out of His tremendous love for us God sent His only Son, Jesus, as a replacement for the punishment for our sins. It was God's dream for mankind. God sacrificed His sinless Son, in our place. When we ask God to forgive us of our sins, because of Jesus' death on the cross, we are forgiven and reconciled to God. God's forgiveness can't be earned by any of our own good deeds, (we do good things because we realize how much He did for us, want to grow in Christ's nature, and want to serve Him and fulfill our destiny), and this can only be received by faith. Because of

Christ's sacrificial love for us we can come to God anytime with anything and relate with Him. We do this by simply speaking with Him from our heart. We must also take time to do some reflective listening as well. Like when I heard God tell me to write. It wasn't an audible voice. But more like a thought whispering in my mind, and a knowing within my being.

As believers and servants of Jesus Christ, He has a special investment in us to fulfill a God-given dream. He called the twelve disciples and told them, "I will make you fishers of men" (Matthew 4:19 NIV). This concept appeared strange to these fishermen. But God had a plan for their lives that would alter their course and bring change and transformation, new adventure, abundance in relationships, financial prosperity, and add purpose and new spiritual meaning to them. He had a dream for them to pursue! Their ordinary lives would become extraordinary! So can ours.

God wants to speak to us, and instruct us in the things we need to know to help our life to be blessed, enjoyable, and filled with purpose and meaning. Learning how to hear from God and being led by the Holy Spirit is one of the most exciting adventures we can embark on. God always desires to help us, but sometimes we miss His help because we fail to recognize Him speaking to us. Like a good parent talking to their children, God wants to tell us the things we need to know to succeed in life. We need the guidance of the Holy Spirit to help us here on earth.

As I spent time with God, I studied and pondered the many ways He communicates with us. I reflected over the years how I had followed God's direction and how He led me.

Spiritual direction and revelation come through 3 distinct sources: our own mind, will and emotions, the Holy Spirit of God, or evil spirits. I ask God to help me discern the difference between His voice, my voice and the voice of our enemy the devil; the devil is the voice that leads us into temptation with negative ideas. He does this by interjecting concepts through our thoughts, and feelings, or from words and ideas spoken to us from someone else. Wrong choices are distractions that can cause the destruction of our dreams.

Discerning the voices speaking to us helps us to distinguish the difference between our own wrong desires and those that are given to us from God. In the past, I've followed desires that weren't from God and they fizzled out on me and left me with regrets of time and energy. As well as consequences I suffered from them. "They hastily forgot His works. They did not [earnestly] wait for His plans [to develop] regarding them" (Psalm 106:13).

The anatomy of a dream starts with the ability to hear from our Lord and allow Him to lead us. We believe we hear from Him through faith. God doesn't have a one size fits all way of speaking. He knows different ways to reach us at different times in our unique differences. "For God does speak-now one way, now another though man may not perceive it" (Job 33:14 NIV).

Here is a list of some of the ways God speaks to us:

Stormy circumstances: These can cause us to search our level of Spiritual maturity. That was the case with me. When I suffered loss I had a strong desire to get closer to God. I started by listening for His voice which I found can be like a soft gentle whisper or a thought that comes from within our hearts: I have never heard God speak to me from an outside audible voice, although some people have claimed to hear from God this way on occasion. The voice of God within us sounds gentle, caring and definitive. It's a positive concept that comes to mind. He doesn't speak to us to condemn us, He only leads, instructs or convicts and convinces us of what we need to do to fulfill his plan. If it is a voice of condemnation the message is not from God. "There is now no condemnation for those who are in Christ Jesus" (Romans 8:1 NIV).

Peace with a decision: Colossians 3:15 says … "Let the peace (soul harmony which comes) from Christ rule (act as umpire continually) in your hearts [deciding and settling with finality all questions that arise in your minds, in that peaceful state]".

When making a major purchase have you ever noticed sometimes you have peace with your decision, other times you don't? That's the Holy Spirit within us acting as the umpire of that decision. It might not be the right thing or the right time. However, we may have peace with buying it another time or we may never have peace about it. God helps us make decisions through a sense of peace.

Our conscious to know the difference between right and wrong: We were created with a conscience so we can discern the difference between right and wrong. Common sense is an example of this and is conventional wisdom given to us by God. He's not going to give us 'free will' to make wise choices without giving us the ability to choose wisely. "... their consciences also bearing witness..." (Romans 2:15 NIV). God leads us through the inner prompting of our conscience.

Night dreams or daydreams: Dreams take us past our conscious beliefs. I have been a vivid daydreamer since I was child. I enjoy sitting and dreaming about what I desire to do or obtain. It is a positive way to use our imagination to think about something we desire to do or see happen. It makes it more a reality and helps our faith work toward the achievement of that dream. Dreams are the desires that come from deep within us. We all have them! Many a man and woman who has a strong idea, invention, call or desire to change something within themselves or help society in some way does so because of a God-given dream. Sometimes dreams are as simple as an improvement in our relationships, or to build a home or send a child to college.

God also speaks to us in nighttime dreams: There are many books written and CD's recorded regarding this topic. I've learned to discern a few vivid dreams that I had while asleep. It was evident to me that God was speaking through them. Not every dream we dream is from God... there's those "Pizza dreams" as we call them. They are the ones that make no sense at all. Then there's nightmares those frightening imaginations injected into our minds through torments or negative thoughts that cloud or minds. A dream from God will lead us to the fulfillment of something good.

I got married at a young age and started a family. After my three children were born I had dreams I needed to return to school. After a period of time, and several of those dreams, I went to college to become a nurse.

"Even at night my heart instructs me" (Psalm 15:7 NIV). That story is found in Chicken Soup for the Soul: Inspiration for Nurses book.

Dreams can release destiny, wisdom, answers and direction. Ask God what your dreams mean. There are books that can help with this, but be cautious, the interpretation of our dream is specific to us because sometimes the symbol means something specific only we can understand and know.

I heard a true story about an inventor of the sewing machine who needed to know how to thread a needle, in a dream he saw an arrow being shot through a cloth and realized that was the answer.

Strong impression or knowing: This is when we know we are supposed to do something, like when I realized I was to return to school. I had dreams at night, but sometimes during the day I'd get the feeling or a knowing that I needed to go back to school. That's one way the Holy Spirit of God is leading and directing. You just know that you know it's the thing to do.

Repetition: Have you ever had a message come to you over and over? When God was directing me to a new church I kept getting invitations from people inviting me to the same church. Two of the people were total strangers to me! I took that as a message and started attending the church. It was the church where I met my husband. Another time, when God revealed part of my life purpose was to life coach others, I kept coming across information on becoming a life coach.

I receive repeated invitations to speak at churches and other events. Those repeated invitations let me know God was guiding me in that direction. There is even messages of repetition in the Bible. I have found the same passages of Scriptures in different places. This proves God repeats messages.

Songs: Music is important to God. It is threaded in events throughout the Bible. When Mary found out she was about to become the mother of Jesus, Scriptures reveal the words to a song she broke out and sang.

I have had direction given to me in the lyrics of songs once or twice. Just at the right time a thought pops into my mind through the words of a song I've heard. I thought it was amazing when this first happened to me. But I realized God has a whole book in the Bible He dedicated to songs called, Song of Songs.

Scriptures: They are wisdom for us to live by. They are God's promises and principles to build our faith and direct us to a blessed life. They contain His wisdom and prophecy. He can speak to us personally through them. (Like the message He gave me to "Go publish!").

Spending time makes His voice recognizable: Several years ago, one of my sons was in a near fatal accident that left him in a coma. Three nights after his accident, I left the hospital exhausted. I had just fallen asleep when a nurse called from the hospital. She informed me Jim had come out of his coma. Receiving that miraculous news, I quickly drove to the hospital. When I entered his room the only light was from the monitors at his bedside. I wasn't sure if he was awake or asleep because the room was dark and his eyes were still badly bruised and swollen shut. So I bent down next to his ear and whispered, *"Hi, Jim this is Mom."*

He wrinkled his face as if perplexed and asked, *"Are you sure?"*

I asked him in return, *"Whose voice does this sound like?"*

A huge grin broke out on his face as he replied, *"My mother's!"*

After years of hearing me speak to him, Jim recognized my voice. As we grow in our relationship with God, we can learn to recognize His soft, gentle voice and the many ways He leads and guides.

Hearing my voice brought my son back to reality...God's voice does the same for us. It helps us realize truth.

Listening to God helps us determine if this dream is really ours. Is it something we really want to do or is it someone's idea we are just going along with and have no desire to do? We've heard the stories about children whose parents want them to take-over the family business but they have another idea in mind and don't want to follow in their parents footsteps. When this happens it may be God is giving them different direction.

When we are passionate about achieving something it could be our dream calling. Jeremiah the Old Testament prophet said his dream was like a fire shut up in his bones. When we feel that same kind of passion stirring in our hearts it will bring us joy to be obedient to act on those God-given desires.

Learning to hear takes time and practice. Ask God a question. Write it down. Then listen for an answer. When it proves itself, you'll know it was God's voice you heard. "Let be *and* be still, and know (recognize and understand) that I am God" (Psalm 46:10).

Hearing from God is something we develop and become skilled at. We never become experts at it; but as our experiences and relationship with Him improve our ability to hear and understand what He is saying to us becomes clearer. We move from one level to another as we mature in spiritual insight and understanding.

Open and closed doors: "What he opens no one can shut, and what he shuts no one can open" (Revelation 3:7 NIV). God is the opener of doors and He also closes them. We need to ask God to open doors no man can close and close doors no man can open to bring us into our destiny.

~ ~

Obedience

Get acquainted with the Father's Love. He's not a hard taskmaster. He's loving, and patient. Obeying God's directives delivers us from the punishment and chastisement of consequences. Obedience to a conviction brings about fulfillment for God's plans and dreams. Disobedience can hinder our destiny by taking us in a wrong direction. God wants to help us fulfill our purpose and destiny. The devil brings destruction through tempting us to disobey. Obeying what He tells us to do will help us implement the plan. "If you are willing and obedient, you will eat the best from the land" (Isaiah 1:19 NIV).

I want God's best...don't you?

God desires our obedience because He has a great plan for us. It's the way we can fulfill that plan and bring that blessing into our lives. I came to realize many times we plot our course, yet we seek God to bless it. I've done that many times in my life and found it's His way that works.

Jesus' first miracle was turning water into wine at a wedding. In order to do so the people standing close by had to fill the six empty stone jars with water. His mother was present and instructed the people, "Do whatever He tells you" (John 2:5 NIV). Mary was a woman of perception and vision. She had experienced a miracle in her own life. She knew acts of obedience would bring about miracles!

I've been published and spoken in places I only dreamed of...only because I obeyed His instruction to me to write, publish and speak.

2

Change - It's the Link to Your Dream

"To every time there is a season, and a time for every matter or purpose under heaven."

~ ECCLESIASTES 3:1

One thing you can count on in life is change. Sometimes change comes for the better. Other times, changes come that are not so good, forced upon us by life circumstances beyond our control. Changes can also come from a choice that is wise or unwise that we ourselves have made.

Some changes we experience are a change in our bodies, knowledge, gifts, skills, talents, values, family, finances, friends, and mates. And then there are the changes that take place within us. Those heart attitudes that develop for either the good or bad and change and mold and shape the way we view things.

Most of us don't enjoy change or view it in a positive way. I have a friend who detests and resists change. But whether we like it or not, change is here to stay. It's a principle established by God. The Scripture in Ecclesiastes 3:1 explains that change moves us into a new season or purpose in life.

We've all experienced change. However, I don't remember being taught much on the subject. How I would have loved to have taken a class on 'Change 101' so I would have had a better understanding of my seasons of change. Through my experiences with change I have learned that it is God's way of prodding us into something new, even a new way of thinking and perceiving what's happening to us. And the only way through change is by making more changes!

Change feels like loss, and oftentimes, it is a loss that brings change. The way we handle change may determine how long we wait for new changes to come. We may need or take the plunge to change ourselves if nothing happens. In my time of great transition I discovered this Scripture in Isaiah 43:18 (NIV) "Forget the former things; do not dwell on the past. See, I am doing a new thing! Now it springs up; do you not perceive it? I am making a way in the desert…" Other translations say wilderness. Loss and change can make us feel like we are in the wilderness. We are in a place we've never been before that feels awkward and uncomfortable. We don't like it and are not sure how to function in this new place. The principles in this book are about how God helps us function in our changes and provides us dreams and visions to make our way. If we can't perceive them right away, we can trust that eventually He will make a way for us to discover them.

Everything can change and everyone can change. Change is personal to our lives. It's about what *we* need to change. Change can bring reward or profit us.

The mental and emotion aspects of change are difficult to handle and process for some…they hold on to tightly to the past. Others deal with it easier. How easily we change depends on our personality types and past experiences.

Changing seasons require patience. Most of us have to grow in that area. It's a test of patience.

Sometimes, we have to be willing to give up instant gratification and comfort to accept change.

Wondering what happened to us is appropriate for a time, but then we need to arise and become proactive and make something happen.

We can learn to discover new purpose in our change. I often prayed, "I cry out to God Most High, to God who fulfills his purpose for me" (Psalm 57:2 NIV). I asked this for every aspect of my life, as a wife, mother, friend, and nurse, etc.

God doesn't cause or provoke every change or bad circumstance that happens, but He will orchestrate a plan and work them out for our good. I believe that's why we have His principles and promises to believe in; they are to help us overcome circumstances. With that in mind, I delved into Bible study during my perplexing season of change.

Change is a great time to work on the part of us that we have overlooked or ignored. In doing so, we must get to know ourselves. Jesus was always asking people questions. This helped them discover awareness for things in their lives that needed to change. When we examine ourselves we awaken and develop awareness to our inner thoughts, outer circumstances and new dreams. Awareness is the first step toward any change. Becoming born-again is all about the awareness and transformation we go through as believers in Jesus Christ. Just as the caterpillar goes through the rough changes or transformation to become a butterfly, we have to go through some rough places to change and grow in our character to fulfill our destiny. The disciples are an example of this. Each of them started changing as they followed Jesus and watched the miracles he performed. The Apostle Paul is an example of an amazing transformation of character. He went from killing Christians, to becoming one, and leading others to Jesus Christ.

Oftentimes, when change makes its way into our circumstances we need to be the ones to initiate changes in our lives to bring us to a better place. I have found that God can use our experiences of change to make us wiser. When we have health, marriage or other problems we read, go to conferences or teleseminars and learn things that pertain to our issues. It teaches us how to handle them. Sometimes we're trying to do things the same old way that don't work, rather than making a necessary change. God is always trying to help us make wiser and healthier decisions. When we gain understanding in our change that's one way God works all things for the good.

Processing our grief is also a significant part of change. I discuss this in another chapter.

Change is a great time for a new beginning. We can't always change a circumstance, but we can change our thinking and viewpoint about it.

Changes may come through the alteration of people, places, things, like the many changes that occurred in my life story; a moment of unexpected change such as the knock at the door brought my husband to me. One call brought sad news and changed my life when I lost a loved one. Another phone call brought forth an amazing change with the sudden appearance of a word processor when I needed one.

Divine moments can change our lives. Responding to them appropriately can bring about miracles. Detours of change can lead to our divine destiny. In my life, over time, I began seeing how the changes I was going through helped link me to a new God-given purpose and dream as a Christian writer and eventually a speaker and nurse, life coach. I found learning new things in my time of change to be challenging, yet, enlightening, inspiring and motivating!

We can ask ourselves a few questions in our time of change and challenge to help perceive and know the season we're in.

What activities do I need to change to move forward.
How can I prepare to move ahead?
What season am I leaving behind.
Am I making excuses to hold me back?
What did I gain during this time of change?

I recently met a woman who at 79 years-old made a major life change. Her husband died and she decided to move closer to where her son lived. This meant leaving a town where she spent most of her life. She packed up and moved to another state. After doing so, she found her dream job in a local hospital as a Chaplin. Her willingness to make a huge change linked her to her dream. She could have allowed emotional ties to excuse her from moving on to where her dream was waiting for her.

Hearing this woman's story reminded me of Naomi, in the Biblical account of Ruth. When it came to change, Naomi found age didn't matter. When her husband and 2 sons died, Naomi instinctively knew it was time for change. Moab, the place where she was living meant, "The place that doesn't require change." She knew a change was in order. She decided it was time to return to her hometown. Her daughter-in-laws wanted to go with her. She told them to stay in their homeland. One of them, Ruth, desired to go with her, and insisted that Naomi's people were her people, and Naomi's God was her God. With Ruth's change of heart, she knew she no longer belonged in Moab. However, Orpah, Naomi's other daughter-in-law decided to stay. Maybe she realized change was too challenging for her. When faced with it she felt the cost of breaking ties with her homeland and it's associations to be too high a price to pay.

Naomi and Ruth found a new life in their change. Ruth found a job with a boss named Boaz. Eventually they married and had a baby who was an ancestor of Jesus. Naomi became a grandmother! They found God is a God of change and purpose.

God can bring purpose and new dreams to anything if we allow Him to. In our times of change we must be patient and wait for new changes to take place. We must allow change to be worked out for the highest good in order to be the link to our dreams.

"And we that in all things God works for the good of those who love him, who have been called according to his purpose." (Romans 8:28 NIV).

3

Rejection - It's a New Direction to Your Dream

"Instead of your [former] shame you shall have a twofold recompense."

~ ISAIAH 61:7

There isn't a person alive that hasn't experienced rejection in one form or another, but most of us have never understood its nature, or the lasting effect it can have on us. Some rejections are relatively minor; others are so devastating they affect our whole life.

Like many of you, I have experienced my share of rejections. However, when I first learned about God's purpose for it, I was sweeping the floor while listening to a Christian radio station. I heard a woman's, soft spoken tone of voice, coming over the air waves say, *"Disappointment is His appointment."* I stopped and pondered my recent disappointments of a diagnosis with a strange illness and my misery over an unhealthy relationship. I wondered, *"God, Could this be true?"*

After that God led me to make some changes. I called off a relationship that wasn't good for me. Within a few months there was a knock at my door. I didn't know it at the time, but my husband-to-be was standing at the other side.

Since that day I've not only learned that "disappointment is His appointment" but that we can turn rejection into redirection. Redirection helps us recover from setbacks. It is the way we rework out mistakes, sins and failures.

Life isn't fair! Major disappointments will come. A door closes to a project you worked hard on, or to an opportunity to pursue your ministry, business or career. A relationship you longed for didn't turn out as you expected. You may have been betrayed or abandoned by a spouse, lover, friend, parent or other. A bad diagnosis from the doctor leaves you feeling frightened, or bewildered wondering, *why me?* These situations can stir up feelings of loss, anger, hurt or despair.

When this occurs we should pray, reflect, and look at how we can be redirected. When I became housebound I thought my life and career were over. But as I allowed God to redirect me, He gave me a new purpose.

Our new direction may not be a person, place or thing but an attitude change. We can't allow our hurts and disappointments to make us bitter, or feel victimized and sulk in self-pity. Nor should we become distrustful and withdrawn, easily hurt or touchy. These are dreams stealers. The Bible tells us, "He has made us accepted in the beloved" (Ephesians 1:6 NKJV)-He meaning, Jesus. God wants us to remember in all of our hurts and rejections He still loves and accepts us. If we're accepted by God that's the greatest acceptance we can have (God's acceptance of us doesn't mean God accepts everything we do, but He always loves us and desires to bring us to a better place than the one we're at). God has a reappointment in His plan for us.

There were times when I was dealing with an illness that I fell short of being able to put into words what my symptoms felt like, or how it affected me. Even when I could, many people couldn't understand my symptoms or what I was going through. I felt lonely in my affliction and rejected. But I had to learn to shake off my feelings of rejection and go on and love in spite of misunderstandings. (Read the Bible account of Job. His friend's didn't understand what he was going through, either).

Sometimes, just the rejection of trying another treatment and failing was more than I could handle. But with a little understanding I learned to overcome the feeling of rejection.

Rejections don't have to be anything major. Even in the little things redirection can apply. As a writer I redirect rejection letters. When I get one I look for places to resubmit my writings to and have had articles published by doing this. I have many acceptances to my writing. But I also have a file full of rejection letters. My writer friend and I, oftentimes, discuss our rejection number. We have said for every 100 submissions we might get a few acceptances. Even though the first two pieces I wrote were published, I've had my share of heartaches along the way. Looking realistically at the rejection number, can give us a boost of confidence...I'll shove it in the folder and keep going. I've heard it said if you're rejected several times, the good news is you're running about average.

We should also redirect our sins and mistakes. To be redirected we ask God to forgive us of our sins, and the people that have come against us. Then we take a new direction.

When your friend gets pushy and pushes you aside, remember she's pushing you to a new and better friend. (Besides, experts say there will be at least 10% of the population that doesn't like us for one reason or another).

I've had times where I've shared a dream with a friend only to be met with discouraging and disparaging words when they expressed to me they I couldn't see how I could achieve that. When this happens stay true to yourself! Don't rely on the validation of others. Stay excited about your dream. When your boss lets you go-know there's a new start waiting somewhere else. Rejection can push you through a new door to another level of maturity, or a different God-given path.

The amazing story of Joseph starting in Genesis 37 is a Biblical account about young boy and his dreams. His brothers laughed and scoffed at his dream. When Joseph's dream was one day fulfilled, he was second in command in Egypt and saved his brothers from a famine in the land. They almost destroyed their own meal-ticket and deliverance.

Jesus was rejected by men when He walked the earth. I enjoy his remedy for rejection, "If anyone will not welcome you or listen to your words, shake the dust off of your feet when you leave that home or town" (Matthew 10:14 NIV). We need to shake off the emotional dust (feelings), of hurt or shame that rejection tries to place on us. The shame spiral of rejection can hinder us from going forward, or make us hide our God-given dream. We think we're bad, when the negative replies from others leave us feeling we're not good enough or ashamed of our ideas or experiences. (At times, I felt ashamed of my illness because other people didn't understand the diagnosis or what I was going through). God doesn't want us to be ashamed of ourselves. If there's a problem we can fix it with God's help. He erases our past and present hurts and mistakes and tells us in John 6:37, "I will never, no never, reject one of them who comes to Me." When someone else rejects you or your dream idea, know what God has placed inside of you. Don't allow their lack of support to shame you and place you in a downward spiral. Being rejected or harshly critiqued by others can leave us feeling at a loss at achieving our dream. If rejection keeps coming we may have to take a closer look at our expectations and see where they may be unrealistic. Over the years of writing rejections and health remedies that have failed, I often reflect if I am realistic with my expectations. When it comes to having realistic expectations and rejections, I think of words beginning with "R". I have come up with a few of my own you may think of some too. For instance, Realistic, Revise, Redo, Resurrect, Reward or Restore. Sometimes I have to be realistic about what I want to see happen and then rework my dreams vision with some new goals or new places to achieve them. Revising can mean a major change is in order. A revision could mean a new Dr. for my physical health, or a different publisher for the type of piece I'm submitting. I may need to redo my business card, website or author bio. When speaking invitations weren't coming, I decided a resurrection was in order, so I planned some events of my own. I recommended the same to a friend.

We have both found it an alternative to waiting for something else. It was just what I needed to resurrect from the disappointments. Rewarding yourself for your efforts helps celebrate each success makes you feel more confident. It doesn't have to be anything big. A movie you enjoy or a relaxing day at the beach, even a hot fudge sundae. Jesus is all about restoration. In the 23rd Psalm it says, He restores my soul." After a rejection, we can renew our minds, desires, and emotions through some prayer, and reflective listening to what God is saying. Also, speaking positive affirmations that boost our courage.

Pray for a strategic plan to overcome your rejection. Gideon did this. The historical Bible book of Judges, chapter 7 reveals how Gideon was going to battle and needed a strategic plan. God revealed to him he needed to decrease his man power because not all his soldiers were meant for battle; they were not effective fighters. Because of this, the larger number could actually cause him to lose the battle. God wanted them to rely on Him and not think they won on their own power. God revealed to Gideon a plan to help him sift through and decide which men were fit for the battle and which ones weren't. God first weeded twenty two thousand men. That left ten thousand. Then He eliminated another seven thousand leaving only three hundred men to win the battle. God's plan was out of the normal realm of thinking. God's the one with the plan for our dream to take place.

Failure can show more about our potential and resilience than we think. Observe many of the great inventors and how they viewed rejection. Henry Ford was a great inventor of the automobile and mass production. I read a quote he was reported to have said, "Failure is only an opportunity to begin again more intelligently." He went broke five times before he succeeded in business. Walt Disney was fired from a newspaper for lack of creative ideas; he went bankrupt many times before successfully building Disneyland. The stories of those who failed in their beginning are endless. One of my favorites is about Steven Scott the author of the book, The Richest Man Who Ever Lived. He was fired from jobs about 9 times. He asked a friend what he should do. The friend instructed him to read through the book of Proverbs. He started to intently study them. He wrote them in categories and applied them to his life. Before long he became an entrepreneur, started his own company, and became a millionaire. We can't allow failure of rejection to make us quit and give up. We need to keep trying until we get it right.

My greatest advice on overcoming rejection is to remember that no man has the right or power to advise you who you are or what you're called to do. Look to our loving Creator and Savior for that advice and affirmation.

4

Write the Vision- It's the Blueprint to Your Dream

"Write them on the tablet of your heart."

~ PROVERBS 7:3 NIV

Everybody has a dream. We need to identify and examine ours. Dreams are God's way to use us to reach out and make a difference in the lives of others.

Dreams provide us with the energy to achieve a God-given goal and motivate us when life's struggles weigh us down.

Dreams add purpose and meaning to our lives rather than living an empty existence.

Dreams draw us into partnership with God and His plan for us. They give insight into our future.

Dreams inspire our creativity, and help us to live an extraordinary life.

Dreams and visions are like small seeds that grow into something greater as they are nurtured with the right ingredients.

God gives us night dreams and daydreams. In this book I'm referring mostly to the daytime dreams we have. You may wonder how we daydream. As a childbirth educator I use to have the parents practice their slow, deep abdominal breathing and dream about their new life as a parent...Now, you, take a moment and a deep breath and let your mind ponder and visualize how your life will change as your dream unfolds.

Dreams and the Creator's steps to fulfill them come from deep within. John 7:38 reads, "Streams of living water will flow from within him" (NIV).

I enjoy the way God explains how we achieve our dreams. "For a dream comes with much business *and* painful effort" (Ecclesiastes 5:3). It takes faith filled effort to believe in them and physical effort to achieve them.

Part of realizing our dream involves identifying God's direction and establishing goals that achieve it. The Apostle Paul mentioned in Philippians chapter 3, "to press on toward the goal." From this Scripture we see the importance of establishing goals. Goals help us achieve our dreams great and small. Goals can be written for personal development, career advancement, spiritual formation, physical health, financial wealth or relational growth. Ideally, we should establish goals in each of these areas.

Studies prove that we are more likely to act on our goals if we have written them out. Even a short "TO DO" list is a good start that can help us establish and take small steps toward a long term goal. A small list makes it feel easier to achieve. Every small step helps toward the accomplishment of our BIG dreams!

Goal writing helps with decision making. By writing out a problem and observing obstacles or solutions in the achievement of it we can identify what works and what doesn't. Goals help us discern the difference between which opportunities are good and which are best for us to pursue. Goals help us view problem solving as a normal process by stretching our ability to use critical thinking skills. Goals give us the realistic perspective to expect to have obstacles and God-given plans to overcome them. This makes us feel more confident because we are taking action to control our lives. The apostle Paul warned us in Ephesians, chapter 6 that we need to successfully stand against the strategies and deceits of the devil. Problems are the devils deceits that hold us back; goals help us overcome them. Our goals need to be authentic to our wishes, desires and the things necessary to fulfill them.

Goals help us keep our focus and accomplish our desires. They take us from where we are to where we want to go. Step by step each goal sets our dreams in motion, and makes it achievable and believable!

Writing the vision helps us identify and overcome when we meet problems or obstacles. It's a way that gives our dream an entrance into our soul (mind, will and emotions), and to carry it through. Writing has been known to have the power to heal, comfort or bring peace to our troubled soul. I believe that's why in my troubling times God instructed me to write.

As a nursing student I learned goal writing is one of the regular steps taken to establish and evaluate a patient's progress. Nurses are some of the best goal writers. When I came across the Scripture in Habakkuk 2:3 "Write the vision," I thought about all the goals I had written for my patients... I was so excited to see it was God's idea all along! Now I see goal writing and planning is the blueprint for achieving anything.

As nurses we refer to our patient's written goals as, "Care Plans"... I believe it's because careful thought and planning goes into the creation of them.

Join in and tap into the power of putting your life on paper. Here are a few pointers when writing goals to achieve BIG dreams...

I like to use the acronym DREAM to give you a basic idea how to plan a goal.

D: *Define and Detail your plan. Make sure your dream goal is concise and specific. Write a detailed vision of the things you want to see develop in your life.*

R: *Reasonable problems or practical obstacles are barriers from making your goal reachable. Look at the things that are hindering you from reaching your goal. Working at a job you're not happy with on the way to your dream job can be a problem due to lack of time to pursue the business you want. Your plans may be altered due to a lack of finances. Sometimes you need more resources if your goal involves a new vocation or business, or to pursue a healthy lifestyle. Once identifying these obstacles, other goals may branch off of your* main goal. Such as identifying the need for finances. A new goal would be necessary once this problem is identified.

Limited knowledge is another problem or hindrance. You're experiencing new things so you need to expand your skill and knowledge base to achieve your dream.

Be aware of fears and limiting excuses that can get in the way. List your fears in this section...in my case, the fear of having my writing rejected could be a problem. Reactions to food or exposure to chemicals is at times an obstacle for me when going forward in my goal for optimal health. Since I live in the Midwest, when it comes to my outside walking, my problem could be problematic weather conditions.

E: Evaluation is expecting an ending. This is necessary for the achievement of your dream goal; otherwise, it is easy to keep delaying putting it in motion. Set target dates or deadlines of completion for each goal. For goals that have a big picture with timeframes in the distant future (like when I went to nursing school), set a target date for its completion, however, start by breaking down your steps into smaller short term goals that you can attain by the day, week, or month. If you don't achieve your goal in your set time, you can change your target date for completion. Sometimes obstacles cross your path and you need to change the date. Looking at my goals to write one hour per day became unrealistic. There were days I was fatigued or had too much pain to write. Other times, household issues such as housework or family demands had to be handled. My goal was unmet and I had to reevaluate and write a more realistic goal.

Another goal I redefined was walking outside for five minutes or more. I was quickly meeting that goal. After that I needed to write a new goal to increase my time or stick with that one and monitor it to make sure I stuck to it on a long term basis!

A: Achievable and Attainable is part of the process in developing a plan. After you've written your goal and the problems you encounter achieving it, you want to come up with a plan or tactic to overcome the obstacles. Start with small steps that you can attain. This will help you put your goal into action ("faith without works is dead" James 2:17).

My goal for my speaking and writing ministry is to start local but expand global. Remember keep your tactics attainable! "I will write at least one hour a day five days a week. I will meditate on healing Scriptures for 15 minutes each morning to build my faith to be healthy and alleviate my fears." You must be practical in designing steps you know are within your ability to reach.

M: Measurable goals are reachable goals. Make your dream something you can measure to make sure you are achieving it. If you can't measure goals you can't meet them. The *results and expected outcome need to be recognizable and recorded. I established a goal to walk outside 10 minutes each day. That was measurable. Did I go outside each day? How long did I stay outside? If I didn't go out, why not? You can see how that was easy to evaluate.*

A few other tips are: Choose goals that stretch and challenge you, but don't break your ability to achieve them or you may get discouraged and quit. I started with small things first. Even going outside my goal was10 minutes to start with. I believe in dreaming BIG, but a BIG dream usually starts with small steps. Enlist someone to keep you accountable. Set up a reward system for yourself to celebrate each goal you obtain.

Another easy way to record your goals is to use a dream calendar. I have used a free calendar and filled in the dates for future presentations I was planning for the year ahead. Then I went back and scheduled the details to make it happen. You can also use it to schedule daily activities you need to do to make your steps work for you. I place each bill I need to pay on the calendar date it is due. It's a simple way to achieve a goal!

Basketball legend, Michael Jordan was cut from his high school basketball team. After that, he committed to a goal he established to shoot 300 baskets a day. Following through with a goal helped his dream become a reality! Yours can too.

Now let's discuss the dreams journey!

— —

Journaling your dreams

Journaling is another facet of writing out our dreams. My first journal was given to me several years ago as a birthday present from a patient I was caring for. The pages within were lined and each contained an encouraging Scripture verse at the bottom. I placed it in a bookcase next to a chair I often sat in for my special prayer time. It remained there unused for quite some time. Then one day, while rifling through my bookcase, I came upon it. When my hand touched it I decided to give it a try. Unsure how to go about it, I started by penning a simple prayer.

Over the years, through varied life experiences, I've come to understand the various aspects of journaling. I found it can be the key to unlock a door to self-discovery and healing.

The Scriptures reveal God does some journal writing of His own. When we are saved our names are written in the lambs book of life (Revelation 20:12). He also records our conversations regarding Him, in a book of remembrance (Malachi 3:16).

In Numbers 33:2 it states, "Moses recorded their starting places, as the Lord commanded, stage by stage". Moses took the Israelites on a journey out of Egypt where they had been slaves for 400 years, and led them into and through the desert toward a land and better life that God promised them. The journey was filled with challenges, great risk taking adventures and experiences. Much like our own journey through life.

I believe the God-given dreams inside our hearts represent our promised land. They take decisions, God-given direction and steps of faith to see them fulfilled. As you read the Biblical record of the Israelites journey you can see the things Moses recorded. He wrote down step-by-step where they went and what they experienced. He even recorded his conversations with God. We realize his dream to lead the Israelites from Egypt came to pass. Through journaling our steps, they can become clear as we write down where we have been and determine where we desire to go. When I read this Scripture I figured if God instructed Moses to journal the journey it must be an important principle; so why shouldn't we record ours?

Another Scriptural basis for goal writing and journaling is found in Habakkuk 2:3, "Write the vision and engrave it so plainly upon tablets that everyone who passes may [be able to] read [it easily and quickly] as he hastens by. For the vision is yet for an appointed time and it hastens to the end [fulfillment]; it will not deceive or disappoint. Though it tarry, wait [earnestly] for it, because it will surely come; it will not be behindhand on its appointed day."

The Old Testament prophet was instructed by God to write his dream or vision down and wait for it to come to pass. It keeps the dream alive while we wait. We are instructed in this passage that the dream or vision has an appointed time. Keeping our dream alive while we wait is important to in order to achieve its fulfillment.

When we are bursting at the seams with new thoughts or dreams the Lord has instructed us to carry through, it's a good time to jot the particulars down on paper and keep them alive so when the devil comes with adverse circumstances that threaten to "steal and kill and destroy" (John 10:10) them, we can go back to our original thought and keep the passion burning.

Journal entries can be used at a later time when writing something greater such as a memoir or personal life story. "My heart is overflowing with a beautiful thought! I will write a lovely poem to the King, for I am as full of words as the speediest writer pouring out his story" Psalm 45 (LB).

King David penned his thoughts and emotions to God. Some examples in his journals include: Psalm 94:19, "In the multitude of my [anxious] within me, Your comforts cheer *and* delight my soul!" Who hasn't had a multitude of anxious thoughts? Take a few moments to express your thoughts in your journal regarding the dreams you believe have been crushed, unfulfilled and broken. Writing out hurts and disappointments is like releasing the toxins that have accumulated in our souls. It reveals what we have been hiding in our hearts. Once we recognize our feelings we can start to work on overcoming them. It helps unravel perplexing problems as we write out the issues that are disturbing us; step-by-step we can uncover the mystery of our problem. When our thoughts are written down on paper it is therapeutic for healing our emotions. If we go for counseling we can share these thoughts with our counselor or we can work with the Counselor, the Holy Spirit within us.

Journaling helps us get in touch with our feelings and is a good spiritual, mental and emotional discipline for cleansing our hearts and minds. It helps our physical and emotional well-being by helping us feel free to express our inner most thoughts and hang ups; doing so can stabilize our moods and trigger the release of hormones such as endorphins, which elevate our moods. When we are in better balance it can relieve muscle tension that can be the cause for backaches, neck or shoulder aches or tension headaches. Cancer patients and others with chronic illnesses have relieved stressful emotions through journaling.

Journaling doesn't have to be labor intensive, complex or intimidating. There are simple and fun ways to journal. Just grab a pen or pencil and write anything that comes to mind.

Journaling is similar to keeping a diary. When I was a young girl it was a cool thing to have a diary. The secret hiding place was under a bed pillow.

Some business people keep a daily record or journal of expenses such as gasoline, or meals. It's used as a log. Other's diary their daily activities to assess how they use their time. I've done this for employers when I worked at hospitals. They requested time studies to ensure we were using our time wisely.

To keep journaling gratifying and meaningful you can journal as much or little as you like. Once a day, week, month, or just when something significant happens. Journaling is appropriate anytime of the day or night.

The time span of recording in my journals is anywhere from several times a day, to every few months or longer. The freedom is there are no hard-fast rules to how it's done or how often you need to do it! I expressed this at a conference where I spoke on the topic of journaling. A woman told me afterward, she gave up her journaling in the past, because she thought she failed at it since she didn't document something each day. This concept set her free!

Dating Scriptures that have personal significance can be a form of journal recording. I place a date next to Scriptures I believe are guiding me. When the Lord instructed me to publish, I was led to a series of Scriptures that confirmed that message to me. I took my pen and placed a date next to each of those Scriptures. Now, I can look back and see the time frame when that took place and how God spoke to me personally through the Scripture pages in my Bible. I'll share a few... Psalm 79, "We will show forth *and* publish your praise… " Psalm 68:11, "The women who bear *and* publish [the news] are a great host".

Clip or save articles in your Journal. One day I opened a magazine and read an article on writing, speaking and life coaching. As I read through it I felt excited about all the things written there. I could connect with them. The moment I read them I knew they were something I was meant to do. Throughout the article I felt God was confirming some of my destiny, and giving me new direction regarding speaking and life coaching. I tore out the page and jotted down the date on the corner and stuck it in my folder. I watched the time frame and how God was instrumental in bringing each new skill and direction to pass.

Writing letters that express feelings and attitudes is something you can add in your personal book. We've all experienced a time of challenge with someone we've cared about. Writing things out can free us from feelings, emotions and issues that we can't seem to let go of and may be delaying our progress. We can practice writing our thoughts and feelings in a letter, expressing how we feel. After venting our feelings we can choose not to send it. But going through the act of writing it out gives us the opportunity to express how we feel about the situation and can often bring some resolution to our hearts. Sometimes we may have to write it several times to feel good the way we expressed ourselves; this improves our communication skills as we get to the point.

Writing our prayers helps bring them to pass. I've heard it referred to by others as the write way to pray! Journaling my prayers is one of my favorite things to do. I pen to God what I am going through and petition my requests. This way I know what I have petitioned God for and can relax and release my faith that He is working on it. The best part is tracking the answers when they come!

Journaling also helps with reflecting listening during our prayer time. It's a way of jotting down what we believe God is instructing us to do. Journaling prayers, insights and their answers helps us to depend on our ability to hear from God and be directed His Spirit.

Writing in our Journal helps track God experiences that enhance our relationship and trust in Him. Whatever you want to call them, God winks, God stops, or God coincidences, journaling them is a way of capturing them on paper so they can be remembered at another time. Psalms 66:5 says, "Come see the works of God" When I'm at a low point in my life it refreshes my faith to reflect on all the wonderful God experiences I've encountered. When I reentered the outside world after being housebound for eight years, I recorded many of my first steps. Journaling this memorialized that treasured moment which took place as I was stepping into my dreams.

The Bible book Malachi 3:16 tells us, "Those who feared the Lord talked often to one another; and the Lord listened and heard it, and a book of remembrance was written..." Our journals can be a book of remembrance regarding answered prayers. God keeps a book regarding our good conversations. Keeping track in our journals can help us remember all the great things he has done for us! I just recorded an amazing answer to prayer in mine yesterday! Now I can go over it for years to come.

Sometimes the things we desire to journal rush quickly though our minds and we're unable to capture them. At times I have written a whole column in my mind within a few short seconds. But I had to be quick because the exact words to express something flowed through my mind so quickly they were impossible to remember. Speaking with other writers I have found it happens to all of us. I've learned to remedy the problem by jotting down a few key phrases or words that might capture the meaning of the thought. When I've been out somewhere and a thought comes to mind, I've used a napkin or any old piece of paper to jot it down. Then I clip it or staple it in my journal later. You can also use a folder to keep loose journal pages in. I've done both so I don't chance losing my precious thought.

At times I enjoy writing by hand rather than on computer. It feels more expressive to me. Besides that way I am in the habit of being able to write something anytime and anywhere. The down side of writing by hand is that sometimes I write so fast and sloppy I can't read what I wrote. When that happens I've lost some of the benefit from writing it down. You may need to try and regain some of your penmanship while you scribble fleeting thought down. You don't have to be good in spelling or grammar when you journal, either. You can write to your heart's contentment and abandon all fears as you release what's in your heart. My friend who is poor in spelling would enjoy this. Sometimes it's good just to write it out and leave it go! It's the act of writing and releasing that's healing.

You can use any type of writing instrument to construct your journal page. A computer, computer notebook, pen, pencil, or high-lighter will get the job done. Sometimes, I just highlight a key phrase in a book or Bible that has a significant meaning. It's fast and easy. Sometimes when making a journal entry, I enjoy using a special pen like the pewter one my grandchildren gave me for Christmas one year with the saying, "All things are possible with God" (Mark 10:27).

A page in a computer file, lined legal pad, plain white paper, post-it-notes, spiral notebooks, and fancy journals can be used. Sometimes beautiful lined journals make us feel special when we sit down to write a prayer. My husband recently gave me a beautiful teal-blue Journal with the word, "Dream" on the cover to record my dreams and desires in.

My recent revelation is to compartmentalize my journaling. I have various subjects I journal on: family, health, career, marriage, gratitude, or significant dreams I have at night, as well as day dreams I want to see fulfilled...I can track them better by logging them in separate journals. That way it is easier for me to find my prayer for that particular topic and write the answers; or I can go back and see my requests without thumbing through the whole journal to find it.

Wonder what to do with your journals? That's up to you. Some people like to take significant parts and write memoirs. If you're concerned with someone reading what you've written, your writings can be kept in a safe place such as a closet, secured box, maybe even under your pillow, just kidding. Protecting your writing can help you to be completely honest with your recordings. Others burn, or shred them after a period of time so no-one else can read them. I've heard that destroying your document can be a way of showing forgiveness or the fact you feel you've completed a season in your life.

Age or gender is insignificant. You're never too young or too old to start a journal. My grandson's first grade teacher started the kid's in his class journaling this year. My grandson is very good at it. He reads to us some of the special things in his journal. What a precious memory to have things that mattered over the years cemented in writing. This activity helps children get in touch with their feelings and teaches them how they can communicate them through writing.

— ⁓

Develop a Visual *Dream* Journal

Journal keeping helps to develop or improve our imagination. Placing photos in our journal can be another way to express our experiences and be creative. I have constructed a dream/ inspiration board. It's a great way to learn how to dream BIG.

Many of the dreams I refer to are our daydreams or things we desire to see come to pass. Some people consider daydreaming "Spacing out" when their mind takes a break from what they are doing and they drift off onto something else, they'd enjoy doing or accomplishing.

Experts say that daydreams help us solve problems and keep us hopeful. They stir our creativity to keep us productive. In this complex technical world we need to take a break from our computers and look out a window (which is what I often did while housebound). This helps us step into in our future. Relaxing and allowing our mind to view a positive picture of ourselves doing something we are passionate about. That is a form of daydreaming.

As a nurse I learned about imagery as a part of the mind, body, and spirit connection taught to cancer patients as an adjunct to their therapy. This activity helps improve their outlook and produce positive thoughts toward their body image and motivate them toward a healthy well-being and outcome. "Set your minds on things above" Colossians 3:2 (NIV). As I mentioned I used it to dream about myself outside of my house.

Dreams transcend more than health issues. They encompass our finances, relationships and the development of our personal character.

Imagery is an important part of fulfilling a God-given dream. It conditions us for success and sets our dreams in motion. Proverbs 29:18 tells us, "Where there is no vision [no redemptive revelation of God], the people perish". Pictures in our minds and elsewhere help us envision our future. Vision is a gift from God. We were created with vision. We enjoy television which uses our visual senses, in the same way an inspiration board inspires our souls through our sense of vision. If we can see it we can do it. That's the reason what we watch on television matters, because images can influence our lives for good or bad purposes.

My great-grandfather was an architect and used blueprints to build churches. It was a visual of what he expected to see. A dream board is our blueprint to our dream.

To imagine is to picture something in our mind before we see the reality of it. "Faith is the evidence of things not seen." Hebrews 11:1.

Our dream is hidden deep within our hearts and fits us to perfection. Like a pregnant woman our dream develops inside of us waiting to give birth to it. A dream board helps us give birth before it takes place. It's kind of like visualizing a baby by ultrasound before it's born. When I taught childbirth classes the mothers-to-be enjoyed sharing their ultrasound pictures with everyone. It brought the concept of having a baby into reality!

A dream/ inspiration board is a positive and creative approach to take the place of and or compliment written goals a person may have toward the achievement of a dream.

A story in Genesis chapter 30:36 is about a man named Jacob. Jacob struck up a business deal with his uncle Laban. His uncle was to give Jacob all the speckled sheep and the black ones, and the speckled and spotted goats. However, his uncle Laban betrayed Jacob and didn't hold up his end of the bargain. So God gave Jacob a creative idea. It's described in Genesis verses 37-39, "But Jacob took fresh rods of popular and almond and plane trees and peeled white streaks in them, exposing the white in the rods. Then he set the rods which he had peeled in front of the flocks in the watering troughs where the flocks came to drink. And since they bred *and* conceived when they came to drink, the flocks bred *and* conceived in sight of the rods and brought forth lambs and kids streaked, speckled, and spotted". In other words He whittled away the bark to show marks he wanted reproduced and the vision caused the sheep to produce what they saw. I think the principle is that if we keep our dreams and vision in sight it helps them manifest in our lives.

I started my dream/inspiration pictures by cutting out home furnishings and cabinets I desired. Sometimes I clipped outfits from fashion magazines and tucked them away in folders. One day while reading a book I found out about a dream board; the idea inspired me, so I expanded and established my dream board. I cut a flap from a cardboard box and started taping photos, pictures and sayings to promote my dreams. I have a photo from my wedding with all our children standing on the alter lighting the unity candle. This is my affirmation to promote family harmony. I have words from magazines such as, "It's all within your reach," to affirm my desires to be a Christian author and speaker and obtain optimal health. A daydream or picture of our dream leaves an important image on our mind.

I heard a story about a man who was bedridden and had a desire to travel the world and preach. During his recovery period he placed a map on the ceiling as his inspiration board. As he lay there every day he prayed over cities and mapped out his course. Eventually he was out fulfilling his destiny.

Whatever you decide to do, discover the joy and the fulfillment of God's purpose for your life as you journal though each page. You don't have to start big, just, dream BIG! Journal your dream and wait to see it accomplished.

Keep in mind gratitude promotes dreams coming true. If nothing else it sure helps us discover more of the enjoyment in life. There were times David expressed gratitude, "Bless, give thanks!" Many people keep gratitude journals. Start on your journey with a small expression of gratitude each day. Write I to 3 things you are grateful for or paste pictures of tangible items on your dream board! Journaling gratitude is a great way to overcome depression or grief. Many grief counselors recommend it.

Do it at the beginning of the day and watch your day start out more joyful. Do it at night and sleep more peacefully as you are not weighted down with burdens but with things you appreciate. Practice journaling for 6 months and see it change your life. Dream BIG! Watch those dream become realities!

5

Turn Your Grief to Joy and Dream

"...your grief will turn to joy."

~ JOHN 16:20 (NIV)

In my story, I mentioned that because of my childhood belief in God's goodness, I was interested in discovering where God was in all of my suffering and adversity. I wondered what He was doing in my life. (There may have been times you, dear reader, may have wondered this too). With this in mind I started studying my Bible intently looking for answers and to become more intimately acquainted with God. I wanted to hear more clearly from Him and know His heart's desires. I didn't realize it at the time, but I found that in our trouble we can both become closer to God and ask our perplexing questions to Him (The Biblical book of Job and Psalms are examples of this). If we close our hearts to His sovereign will we will never experience His healing from our anxieties and fears. When we share openly with God and invite Him into our fears and disappointments, healing can begin.

One day while in was in prayer, pouring out my hurt and pain, I opened my Bible to come across these 2 words, *"God grieved" (Genesis 6:6)*. I thought, *"God...You have emotions like me!"* After this I paid attention to the emotions I was suffering. Isolation, fear, anxiety, sadness, hurt and depression had become my daily companions. To overcome them I felt God was directing me to get out of bed each day and plan a healthy daily routine, regardless of my circumstances. Doing this helped me from becoming stuck where I was and moved me forward toward my new daily routine.

Through my trial of losses I realized God was bringing me a deeper understanding of how emotions work and how I could get in touch with mine. Through my reading of Scripture passages and insightful books I realized God placed our emotions inside of us to guide us to wise choices and motivate us in a positive way. I discovered they either support or sabotage dreams.

I started looking at what I learned in nursing school about grief and connected it to the emotional responses I was feeling regarding my losses.

Grief is a process that we go through to overcome sadness or despair when we've experienced a traumatic loss. The loss can result in a broken dream that's in need of repair or a new direction altogether.

When we've had a traumatic loss of some kind it stirs an emotional response within us, oftentimes, leaving us feeling sad, depressed, and anxious, overwhelmed, or bewildered wondering what happened or why it occurred. It can stir a whole bunch of negative feelings and thoughts within.

Grief can accompany any kind of loss and is a normal part of human response. Most people think of grief in response to the death of a loved one; but losses of various types can evoke a response of grief to one degree or another.

Common and obvious losses that promote a grief response are that of a friend or family member through death, divorce or separation. Many people have difficulty when they lose a pet. The loss of a job or career we invested ourselves in can leave us in shock when we're given a 2 week notice or our health issues keep us from performing our jobs. Material possessions that have been lost, stolen or repossessed can also produce this response. Disease that threatens our health and well-being, and alters our ability to live a normal productive life, can also leave us in a grief-stricken state of mind.

There are other losses that are more abstract in nature, because they are personal to us and unseen or recognized by others. Yet, they evoke a grief response. These losses arise when our expectations are unrealistic or unmet in some way; they occur when we experience a hurt or disappointment, when we can't live up to someone else's or our own expectations. This also occurs when we have an identity or mid-life crisis, or a deep regret of some kind. These losses wound our souls and make our hearts heavy when they go unresolved.

Any or all of these losses can cause us to feel discouraged and disappointed and hopeless from ever achieving our dreams.

Grief affects all ages. Even children grieve. I recall in fourth grade when my friend for 3 years moved away. I was sad and missed her; I didn't understand why she had to move to another town. I also didn't understand the sadness I felt was due to the fact I was grieving the loss of her relationship to me. I only knew I missed her and couldn't do anything about it.

When grieving takes place we need time to process the loss that occurred. There are many theories on how we overcome grief. In nursing school I learned about Elizabeth Kubler-Ross phases to grief. She was the pioneer in discovering patterns people go through in response to loss. Her scientific studies regarding the death and dying (any type of loss is a death), helps us navigate what to expect when we've suffered a loss. They are not a rigid formula that happens in an exact order, but guidelines or a way to look at and identify what we are feeling during our times of grief. Her model helps us recognize feelings that are a normal part of the process. Although there are many new models for processing grief, most of them are founded on the principles she established. I personally found her phases helpful when I went through my times of loss and transition.

She noted that we, oftentimes, process our feelings in 5 stages: Shock, Denial or Disbelief, Anger, Bargaining and Acceptance.

In the Shock stage we can't believe or understand what just occurred. Especially when a loss happens suddenly. In our state of emotional shock we start going over and over what happened and try to figure out why. Sometimes, there might be something we have done to cause an incident and we need to make a change. Most times we're a victim of circumstances that no amount of questions can answer. Only God has the answer. In this case all we can do is place our trust in Him as Proverbs 3:5 instructs us to trust in the Lord with all our heart and mind and not to rely on our own understanding. We have to direct our thoughts about the occurrence to God and His divine wisdom.

The next stage is Denial; Disbelief or denial is manifesting when we refuse to accept what has happened. We deceive ourselves believing that this isn't really occurring.

"This can't be happening to me," we sometimes chide ourselves. Sometimes the denial is so strong it goes deep to the subconscious level and we act as if the loss has never occurred. Often, it's such a traumatic and unexpected change it takes time to believe what took place. Eventually we must face what has happened and, "forget what lies behind and strain forward to what lies ahead" (Philippians 3:13).

In the Anger stage we feel angry over what happened. "Why is this happening to me? I don't deserve this!" are some of the thoughts we might have. The emotion of anger is not a sin. It is a normal response we have when we perceive our dream has been shattered or our worth and value have been threatened. It can be a response to a blocked goal or dream. It is a defense mechanism to identify the enemy's challenges. It can energize us to move forward if don't allow it to fester. We must express it in an appropriate way. People often get angry at God and blame Him. But that is counter-productive; we need God's help and healing. Talk with Him about it and ask for His help. It can be unhealthy and turn into sin when it becomes destructive and causes us to damage property, hurt ourselves, or others. ("In your anger do not sin," Ephesians 4:20 NIV). Eventually we need to forgive the situation and allow our misery to lead us into a new direction. The longer we stay angry the more destructive our anger becomes. We need to work through the situation and use it for good. Scripture is clear that God is our vindicator. The anger can also be internalized and cause us extreme sadness or depression. I found that reading the Psalms helped me process these feelings. David was often expressing his grief through his descriptive feelings of sadness, depression or anger. Physical symptoms or fatigue can manifest if the anger, depression or sadness get to overwhelming. Taking care of your physical needs of getting extra rest, exercise and eating a healthy diet can help with this.

In the Bargaining stage we try to bargain with God, "I'll do anything to change this." Having an honest dialog with God is always good. Bargaining doesn't always get us what we want, nor do we want to make promises to God we can't keep. When we bargain we're trying to reason with God. But we are informed to "Be not wise in your own eyes" (Proverbs 3:7). It's better to accept God's will and move on. In the bargaining stage we can also have great feelings of sadness we are trying to resolve.

The last stage is Acceptance. This is when we start to take a look at our losses and see what we can do to get a healthy perspective on them. We accept what has occurred and realize we must move forward into God's plan for our lives.

Some people skip over a stage or more. Sometimes, we stay stuck in one stage longer than the others. At times we go back and forth through the stages. Others move through the process quickly. I know this from personal experience when I've had to overcome the grief of losing my family, friends, health and other losses. At times, I got stuck in one phase for a while. Sometimes there was a stage or two I never experienced. Other times I may have processed through a phase only to go back into it again when a the memory of a loved one's birthday or holiday celebrations brought me back in time and triggered a response I thought I had overcome.

There is no right or wrong way to navigate our path to overcome grief. It's an individual process. It depends on what type of relationship we had to the person, place or thing. How we've processed our feelings of grief in the past can also make a difference because we recognize what we're feeling and realize we have gotten through it before; this may help us resolve it quicker. When our losses are compounded, (I lost my health, career, income, and family members), we can feel overwhelmed. When this is the case, it may take us more time to process grief. However, learning to process our thoughts and emotions can help take us from the state of feeling overwhelmed to a state of feeling more confident and empowered as we start gaining control. Talking things though with a trusted friend, counselor or group of others that understands can help vent those feelings of sadness so they don't build up and form a mental attitude of being a victim for the rest of our life. Unresolved grief can cause us to stay angry and blow up at an improper place or time. We can find God's comfort in the scriptures.

Having a good cry can help release pent up feelings. I learned as a nurse that stress hormones such as cortisol are released in tears related to stress and sadness. Allowing those tears to flow can help increase endorphins the feel good hormones. Stress tears are different than tears from peeling onions. Those tears just cleanse the eyes.

Experts state that statistics have proven when someone has the support of family, friends, counselor or even a support group they can recover quicker and better. Leaning on God's Holy Spirit to counsel and comfort in grief, through the study of Scripture passages on God's love and comfort and making them into healthy affirmations can help us move through each stage of grief and find a new starting place.

Following the steps in this book can help reappoint us to God's new, and joyous dream for us. On our journey keep in mind grief is a healthy process. Looking at our emotional responses and processing the phases of grief can get us to a place where we can reach a healthier perspective regarding our losses. As we reflect on our feelings and emotions we can move past the painful feelings of broken-dreams.

Be kind and patient with yourself as you go through the process. As we allow ourselves to feel each phase and work through the pain by expressing our feelings about what has happened, we take steps to move forward to a new place in our life and are able to dream again.

6

Manage Your Emotions and Take Charge of Your Dream

"But be transformed by the renewing of your mind."

~ ROMANS 12:2 NIV

I prayed out of desperation, *"Lord, please transform my thinking! Change my thoughts from fear, doubt and unbelief to confidence, faith and trust."* When I prayed that I hadn't come across this passage of Scripture on transforming my thinking yet. I was just tired of dealing with the same old thoughts that defeated me from making progress in my health or enjoying life. These negative thoughts regarding my situation haunted me, *"Nothing ever changes; Will I ever get well? Every day is the same."* I found it interesting I was becoming more aware of the thoughts that stirred and produced emotional responses in me. I hated feeling afraid things wouldn't get better. I felt like my thoughts were trying to defeat me from moving forward toward my dreams for my marriage, career and financial blessing.

Then I read the book, "Battlefield of the mind," by Joyce Meyer. I learned something I never knew before; I discovered that the devil uses our thinking to tempt and defeat us. He interjects a wrong thought through a negative word spoken to us by someone ("such as you're ugly"), or a word whispered into our minds by him, ("you can't do that"). Like my thought, "Things will never change." The thoughts trigger an emotional response such as fear or anger, and produce an attitude causing us to like or dislike something. The attitude brings about an action, we either say or do something positive or negative. When I discovered this information I realized it was just what I had been asking God for. I was tired of my self-defeating thoughts. I thought whatever I was thinking was a reality, I didn't know my own thoughts could be deceptive, and that I had the power to change them! That's why living the Christian life is considered one of power and transformation. When I looked back on my life, it made sense to me. I recalled how many times God helped me to reshape my thinking about a situation. It was part of transforming my thinking.

I knew that changing our thinking was vital to our mental health, however, I didn't know how to make that change. Then while house-bound, during my expanded Bible study time, I discovered how God created our minds to think, and process calling our unhealthy thoughts, "arguments, and theories, and reasoning's," (The arguments and the reasoning's he is referring to here are regarding our human attitude to argue and reason away Biblical truths with our excuses and wrong perceptions). Instead we are instructed to take every thought captive and cast down the wrong ones and replace them with positive truth from Scripture (My paraphrase for 2 Corinthians 10:4). By studying the Bible we get insight as to what is the right and wrong way to view things. Jesus was always teaching the correct way to handle a situation. His parables grow our knowledge on how to handle situations; they also teach us how to hear from God (as I mentioned in an earlier chapter), and follow His leading on how to think and change a situation.

Since our thoughts stir up emotions and behaviors, when we start imagining wrong things we need to notice the thoughts we are entertaining. Negative thoughts and emotions can impair our ability to think and perceive clearly. They can build prejudices in our lives or perceptions of self-defeat and dysfunction. That's why we can't trust our feelings. Sometimes they support us, like when we start a new job, enter a new relationship or purchase something new... at first it feels good. But eventually the emotional high of a new situation wears off. That's when Satan brings in the feelings of drudgery or dread. Despite these feelings we still need to remain working at the job that was once new and exciting. We need to remain in the challenges and work out the issues of the problematic relationship with our new spouse, even though the loving feelings have subsided.

Other times, we desire to live a better life, but we remain in a frustrating situation. We stay in jobs that drain our strength and energy because they don't challenge our skill or thinking level. We remain in them because we're afraid to step out of our comfort zone. We come home to unhealthy relationships with issues that never resolve, because we are too afraid to confront them.

Strong emotions can feel overpowering and cloud our decision making abilities. When our feelings are hurt we may feel badly bruised and beaten; but that doesn't mean we are, or can't shake those feelings loose. We may have failed at something, or been through a tough circumstance, but we are not a failure, even though we feel like we are.

Demons of shame, humiliation, discouragement, worry and anxiety keep us in defeated patterns because we follow those thoughts and feelings, rather than breaking free from the feelings and trying something new. Shame is the devils destructive force that keeps us bound in the dark because we are too ashamed to discuss our problems and come to some resolution of them. Challenging a negative thought and replacing it with a positive one helps us challenge and overcome an area where we are weak or deceived. It's better than hiding behind a deception and standing still in a destructive mindset for the rest of our life. We can hide behind our delusional thoughts and damaged personalities doing things we believe make us feel secure; but in reality are a false sense of security. We can turn to God for help and look at the truth, or we can become a victim to our circumstances and never discover the life God prepared for us to live. Working with God's Holy Spirit to process and transform our thinking, we can stop living in the false comfort of defeating behavior patterns.

Facing our emotional journey is the beginning of fulfilling a dream. When the reality that our emotional baggage could cause us to destroy our dream for our marriage, finances or health we can challenge our thought patterns and change our lives.

Understanding what normal thinking is helps us identify when we are abnormal. As born-again believers Scripture informs us we have, "the mind of Christ" but we have to develop this mind.

A family member recently shared with me how they couldn't sleep at night for years due to thoughts racing through their mind. When I asked why they hadn't shared this information with me before, they said they thought it was normal. This led me to realize that most people don't know what a normal mind is like. As a nurse with some background in behavioral health I knew what psychiatry considered a normal mind, but with further Bible study I learned what God's view of a normal mind is. I realized a normal mind was God's intention all along.

We all possess areas in our thinking patterns where our mind is un-healthy. Here are a few common examples. A peaceful mind is free of anxiety and worry. Scripture tells us, "Do not fret or have anxiety about anything, but in every circumstance and in everything, by prayer...make our wants known to God" (Philippians 4:6). So the spiritual answer to anxiety and worry is prayer. However, we may have to train our minds not to worry, by casting down the thoughts and replacing them. I'm still working on this too!

Keeping our focus on what we are doing is another sign of a healthy mind. "Keep your foot [give your mind to what you are doing]

(Ecclesiastes 5:1). We live in a world of multi-tasking. Although a certain amount of this is necessary, I don't know one mother who hasn't multi-tasked, we should keep our minds on the main thing we are doing. ("Set your minds" Colossians 3:2). The texting while driving issues are an example of how this is becoming a problem in our modern day world. It causes the mind to wander, therefore, predisposing accidents and mishaps to occur.

The key to change is asking God's Holy Spirit to help us have an awareness of our wrong thinking patterns, and to help us overcome them. (One of the characteristics of the Holy Spirit is that He is our Helper John 14:26). Next, understand that a fearful thought is at the root of every negative emotion we possess, and that as we challenge those unrealistic fears we can break free from the things that bind us. What a life changing concept!

When I was in nursing school, I was required to take a speech class. I didn't know God created me an extravert, who was acting like an introvert, because I was very quiet and timid. The last thing I wanted to do was get up in front of a crowd of people and speak. I put the class off until I had to take it or I couldn't finish school. So, I signed up for the course, and every speech I gave was done in fear and trembling. I recently attended a conference at the same college. The guest speaker's topic was on career changes and advancements. While he was discussing how to promote yourself as the right candidate for a job, a young man from the audience raised his hand and asked the question, *"How do you overcome the fear to do that?"* The speaker replied, *"You don't always feel confident. Sometimes you just do it in spite of your fear."*

If I hadn't done that I wouldn't have completed my dream to become a nurse, or a speaker/ teacher. Fear is a powerful emotion that can rule us if we allow it to. Fear keeps us back from being our best. We believe we can't do something so we don't even try to do anything. Who hasn't felt fearful? Those emotions will cause you to tremble, sweat and to shrink back from doing what you need to do. But I learned from the Bible, "For God did not give us a spirit of timidity (of cowardice, of craven and cringing and fawning fear), but [He has given us a spirit] of power, and of love, and of calm *and* well-balanced mind *and* discipline *and* self-control" (2 Timothy 1:7).

Eventually I was able to overcome some of my fears by doing things regardless of the feeling of fear. As a writer I make submissions regardless of the fear of rejection. To get well I've had to fight my fears of reactions and try new foods, and supplements to move forward in my health. It took me six months to take a whole capsule of a new supplement, because I have to start low and go slow...but I did it!

It can help us if we keep the popular acronym for fear, **F**alse **E**vidence **A**ppearing **R**eal in mind when thinking a thought that produces fear. This popular acronym claims that most of our fears are unfounded and most won't occur. I'm sure we can all look back at some things we did while feeling afraid, and yet succeed in life. The popular saying proved to be true.

Choosing the right attitude can make us feel differently about the people around us. Jesus instructed us to love our enemies.

When feeling depressed or hopeless redirecting that negative thought can take us from hopeless to hopeful in a split second. I had to fight against allowing the feeling of depression and hopelessness while housebound; making myself keep a daily routine regardless of how hopeless I felt was the only way I was able to get out of bed and face each day. "Arise (from the depression and prostration in which circumstances have kept you-rise to a new life)!" (Isaiah 60:1). I spoke this verse to myself daily...sometimes several times a day. Speaking it out loud works even better!

Meditating on this passage helped keep my emotions and focus in balance. It helped me keep up my daily routine, making me feel like I was still participating in life.

Meditating on healing Scriptures such as this one several times a day, "For I will restore health to you, and I will heal your wounds, says the Lord" (Jeremiah 30:17), helped to keep my faith for my healing.

Unhealthy thoughts and emotions can sabotage our dreams. Proverbs 23:7 states, "For as he thinks in his heart, so is he." This shows how we view ourselves can make a difference in achieving our desires. If we view ourselves as a failure chances are we will fail!

At first, when you choose to think positive your feelings and emotions may deceive you. They may feel opposite of your choice because your emotions haven't caught up with your thoughts, yet. Your feelings may linger behind but will eventually catch up.

Negativity affects our creativity. Jesus had a ministry to fulfill. He knew how to manage His thoughts and emotions in order to get the job done. He replaced his negative thoughts with positive ones. He had many creative miracles to perform and positive conversations to pursue.

As nurse I've learned medical science has proven a negative attitude can have an adverse effect on our health. The research on how stress affects our physical well-being is proof of this. Most of the illnesses that exist are stress related. But God gives us a remedy, for our stress that's where the Scripture verse in Proverbs 17:22 explains, "A happy heart is good like medicine... but a broken spirit dries the bones". However, this doesn't mean we should never have a good cry. Crying has been known to release stress hormones produced by stressful situations. That's why allowing the teardrops to occasionally fall can cause you to feel relieved too; sometimes, afterwards you fall into a peaceful sleep.

It is also proven that physiological changes in our bodies can affect our thoughts and emotional stability; side effects of some medications can cause anxious or depressed thoughts and feelings, hormone imbalances such as PMS or menopause can do the same. Even our daily diet, such as adding too much caffeine or sugar can have an effect on how we feel. It can sometimes be more challenging to manage our emotions in these times. But it can be done.

Spiritual disciplines help connect us to the heart of God. I'd like to help you look at some positive perspectives from the Bible on this. Learning these time tested truths about transforming our thinking has helped me to learn how to overcome emotional obstacles. If we redirect our thoughts and values our BIG dreams can be realized. Here are some positive attitudes and affirmations that can bring new possibilities to your life and help fulfill your dreams:

Gratitude: Without gratitude we block our ability to receive God's abundance. Practicing a grateful heart can open doors for insights and revelations and bring possibilities we haven't seen before. Showing gratitude to God and others, makes way for greater blessings to appear. Our constant complaining clouds our vision for the good; and an act of giving conquers bitterness and is a subtle form of gratitude.

"Let us come before him with thanksgiving," (Psalm 95:2 NIV). Expressing a simple "Thank You" to God each day, even when we don't feel there's much to be grateful for, shows Him we're still open to His plan and creates an anticipation for a better future.

I have found making a mental note or writing down three things I am grateful for each day, (as mentioned in my previous chapter) can help us develop a greater trust in God.

Gratitude helps us overcome depression as it deepens our appreciation for God and life.

We should let others know how grateful we are for them in our lives. Let's get creative in our quest for gratitude. It may open a door for new friendships and a whole new way of life. "Seek and you will find; knock and the door will be opened to you" (Matthew 7:7). A simple act of gratitude can open the doors to your dream!

Compassion: A compassionate person puts themselves in someone else's place and shows mercy toward them. Many a dream has been visualized when the dreamer has suffered and overcome a hardship. Their struggle helped them develop compassionate hearts toward others challenged by the same obstacles.

Many businesses have started due to compassionate owners who have visualized a service to meet the need of someone else. God-given dreams should include serving others or making the world a better place with your product or service. God created us to create a dream come true this way, "Show mercy and compassion to one another" (Zechariah 7:9). I started writing things I learned through my challenges to help others know and understand how to cultivate a deeper relationship with God, and navigate their way through difficulties and use them to pave the way to fulfill His purpose and destiny for their lives.

Forgiveness: It's important to extend forgiveness to someone or something that has hurt us. Unforgiveness hurts our lives and destroys the possible repair of a relationship. Sometimes, we can't go back into a relationship, but forgiving what was done gives us a new vision, and letting go of the hurt and disappointment gives us a brighter outlook as we partner with God to fulfill our hopes and dreams. A forgiving attitude keeps us from becoming bitter and angry. It's healthy for us and sets us free. (... "Forgive each other." Ephesians 4:32).

The greatest act of forgiveness was when God extended His only Son to die on the cross for the punishment of our sins. Since God has forgiven us, and paid the penalty of our sins we should extend the same kindness to another. Psalms 103 says, "He forgives all my sins."

Forgiving another is an act of kindness to ourselves as well. I like to say, "To forgive is to abundantly live!"

Trusting God: We decide who or what to place our trust in. We must learn to place our trust in God. We know He has helped get us where we are and we can trust Him to get us to a better place.

There are certain feelings that help us identify whether we are trusting. Trust isn't feeling unsettled, anxious, frightened or agitated. When we really let go, we are trusting God to take control of our life and discover peace and joy that trusting can bring.

The questions to ask yourself is, "In whom or what have I placed my trust?" Are you trusting in yourself, someone close to you, your qualifications, schooling, money or who you know? These things can change throughout our life and often do. We need to trust in God, Who never changes. We can trust God has a plan for our life and can fulfill our dreams.

Upbeat Music: When I was in nursing school one of the healing modalities taught to us was music therapy. Music can sooth our souls and heal wounded hearts. Put on some upbeat music and experience a mood change. Melancholy music can cause us to feel downcast or depressed. If you want to have a good cry that's the kind of music to play. Classical music can stir your creativity. When your creativity needs a boost, try a little 'elevator music' to bring you to new heights and creative insights.

Music can help us overcome depression and has been known to heal our bodies. Music minsters to our emotions and can evoke emotional healing through the words or melody to a song. Music is one of the ways we praise and worship God. Throughout the Bible there are examples of songs that were played and sung to God. The Psalms were actually a collection of music and lyrics. "I will sing and make music" (Psalm 57:7 NIV). Listening to music, or singing a song can motivate you to achieve your dream.

Speaking words of life: There's nothing like a compliment to lift your spirit. Whether read from a note or spoken, a word of praise causes your confidence to rise and keeps you going in the right direction. When we hear negative words spoken to us, they begin to make us feel depressed and discouraged. Even when we speak them to ourselves, we start feeling miserable or defeated. A pleasant word makes us feel victorious or confident. In ancient Biblical days it was customary for the father to speak a blessing-or a compliment-over the firstborn son's life. The parent would speak words that declared prosperity, health and success. The Spiritual tradition was so important that the account recorded in the book of Genesis, chapter 27 reveals how Jacob deceived his father into thinking he was his older brother so he could receive the customary blessing. A kind word spoken about ourselves, to ourselves also nurtures a healthy emotional well-being and keeps us motivated to fulfill our dreams.

When confronting another, do it with kindness. "Be kind and compassionate." Ephesians 4:32. Building others up with our words is one way of showing we care. Even a reprimand should be presented with a positive affirmation included.

We see the effect words can words can have over our soul and spirit. Over a period of time, they can make a difference in our worth and value in a positive or negative way. We need to remember to choose our words wisely and speak a compliment to ourselves and others each day. When Jesus was tempted by the devil, "Jesus answered, It is written" Matthew 4:4 NIV). He quoted Scripture back to him, to affirm the truth.

I've transformed a few powerful Scripture verses into affirmations to help you on your way!

I have worth and value...God loves me!

God is restoring my health and healing my wounds (Refer to Jeremiah 30:17).

God has plans for me for welfare and peace, good and not evil (Refer to Jeremiah 29:11).

I can do all things through Christ who gives me strength (Refer to Philippians 4:13).

I am more than a conqueror through Christ (Refer to Romans 8:37).

Nothing can separate me from the love of God (Refer to Ephesians 1:6).

I am blessed wherever I go...I am blessed when I come in and blessed when I go out, (Refer to Deuteronomy 28).

7

Use Old Skills and New Skills to Discover and Launch Your Dream

"All who are skilled among you are to come and make everything the Lord has commanded."

~Exodus 35:10 NIV

et nothing go to waste...review your life experiences and your skill mix to reach your full potential. Recognizing and using your skills will take you from dreaming to doing. Ecclesiastes 10:10 says, "If the ax is dull and its edge unsharpened, more strength is needed but skill will bring success." Sharpen your tools. Transfer old skills and existing skills, as well as learning new ones. Try something different it may lead you down a new path.

Jesus took a few fish and loaves of bread and fed 5,000 people. There were even leftovers. He instructed the disciples, "Gather up now the fragments (the broken pieces that are left over), so that nothing may be lost *and* wasted" (John 6:12).

What I learned is we can transfer skills and wisdom from the fragments of our past as we move forward. As a nurse I had to write on patient's progress each day. I transferred writing skills to expand in other areas for my writing.

As Childbirth instructor I transferred skills: Teaching, Speaking, Marketing, Coaching.

I use my skills from preparing patient care plans to helping formulate plans for my clients when I life coach.

When the Biblical, King David, was in his transition from Shepard boy to king of Israel, he volunteered his services to help slay the giant Goliath that was threatening to take their land. To give his approval, King Saul supplied David with the usual suit of armor. But David let him know that he didn't desire to use the typical armor the soldiers wore; he had a secret weapon of his own- he possessed a special skill that he had acquired over his years as Shepard and felt readily prepared to slay this giant with his acquired skill. He let Saul know that he had slain many a bear and lion with his old skill of protecting the sheep. He was ready to protect Israel from this opposing giant with five smooth stones and a slingshot! (This is my paraphrase the actual story is found in Samuel 2 chapter).

David's story of slaying Goliath is also an example of how he was willing to embrace his uniqueness. He was proud of his skill and technique for fighting. It wasn't that David was too proud or being stubborn, he just knew inside of himself that he had to do it his way.

We, too, can slay giants in our lives utilizing old skills from our past. We don't have to waste anything.

Learning new skills helps too. Preparation is extremely important in fulfilling a dream. Oftentimes, we enter into a dream with high expectations but no preparation. I've heard this described as "dream limbo." You can have your plan, but without preparation you can't fulfill your plan. The parable of the wise and foolish virgins in Matthew 25:1 depicts this. There were ten virgins. Five of them were wise, the other five foolish. The wise ones prepared ahead of time by filling their lamps with oil...the foolish ones put it off and were eventually left out of the kingdom. Why be left out from fulfilling your dream? Instead, prepare to prosper...I couldn't become a nurse without first preparing by attending college and gaining the knowledge to become one. Our new dream may require some sort of preparation....a class in computers technology to reach out and start a website or a BLOG. I had to learn how to make submissions, e-mail, and other computer skills as well as how to write a book proposal in order to become a professional writer. For my health I had to learn about non-traditional medicine treatments, and supplements and other types of medications I hadn't learned about in order to help me. I had to learn how to reduce environmental toxins in my environment.

Skills can increase our health, pay the bills, and improve our communication. Becoming skilled is the difference between being a professional or an amateur. There are many new skills we can learn to add to our old set. Even when we're stuck between the need for a daily job and our dream one, new skills can temporarily pay the bills while we work at one job to afford our dream or daily needs, and work another that fulfills our dream. Many a couple has destroyed their marriage because one of them quits a job to pursue their dream, while the other works to keep the household afloat. This arrangement can only be entered into with agreement. Even working a part-time job while pursing your dream job can bring cash to help build your dream; it can help you increase socialization skills that to connect you to your dream. Don't be so quick to become a starving artist so to speak. Use financial wisdom when pursuing your dream.

People skills helps us build lasting relationships, heal our families and mend broken hearts, they build character and wisdom for us to succeed. I had to increase my communication skills as a writer. As a nurse, I also needed communication skills to interact with patients and doctors. Most people don't know or realize that part of nurses training is psychology and communication. That's why nurses make great life coaches. We understand mental illness and behavioral issues that can hold someone from a healthy lifestyle. We have the communication skills to coach as a successful counselor. I have found many of my past nursing jobs have given me the experience and skill to do what I do today. God can use every skill great and small.

In your prayer time start asking God if there are there are more skills you need to learn. One of my favorite Scriptures to encourage me to acquire skill is Proverbs 22:29, "Do you see a man diligent *and* skillful in his business? He will stand before kings; he will not stand before obscure men." Kings can represent a prominent person such as a boss or someone you need in your life to help you succeed at fulfilling your dream. The combination of your skill and their need can move you forward.

Succeeding in life is about living your life with purpose as you impact the world with your unique God-given gifts, abilities and talents. It involves the specifics of what you want to succeed at. If you're struggling to discover your purpose it might help if you ask God to help you connect the dots. The dots (as I like to call them), are your past experiences and skill mix. Watching how God has guided your life to where you are now, may give you some clues as to what you are meant to do in this season. I recently discussed with someone how God used my childhood experience with a science fair project (which wasn't even my idea, my teacher assigned it to me!), to shape my interest in the area of childbirth. Amazing how that project in fifth grade caused me to become fascinated with the process of birthing. Then, as a nurse I worked in O.B. for some years and became a childbirth educator at a hospital for 17 years (I'm still a childbirth educator. I now help people birth dreams and also help couples on a one-to-one basis prepare for childbirth). See how God stirred and shaped that desire. It also gave me a strong desire for motherhood- which resulted in conceiving and birthing 3 sons. I've enjoyed the skill of helping others to give birth and become mothers, and now consider myself a spiritual mother as I help and coach others to discover their purpose.

Beyond that, I see how God opened doors for my leadership gifts as a nurse manager. It wasn't anything I pursued. My boss recommended I apply for a management position that was open. At first I didn't think it was right for me; but after praying about it I gave it a shot and the door opened. What I learned from that managing job helps me manage my own business. When I worked at the clinics I was also involved in community health. I set up health fairs in public places and spoke at local schools for career day and various other health related topics. This experience, as well as, teaching my childbirth classes gave me the experience for public speaking and the knowledge to set up my book table for book signings and handle myself in a professional and organized manner. My desire for spiritual wisdom and Bible study coupled with my background as a Sunday school teacher, gave me the desire to become a congregational health nurse. With my background in business and nursing it fits together perfectly to form my desire to inspire people to live fulfilled lives and birth God-given dreams through my writing, speaking, coaching, nursing and Bible teaching. My friend was amazed my path was so clear; the only thing is that I had to inform her it was only clear to me in hindsight. I had no idea all my skills and experiences would fit together to fulfill the functions necessary for the completion of my newly discovered purpose and dream. The day I had that epiphany, connecting the dots of my skill path, cemented my current purpose and dream. That's why I suggest connecting the dots with your past skills and see if you can discover what you were created to do in this season of your life. Proverbs 3:6 proclaims, "He will direct *and* make straight *and* plain your paths."

Jesus grew up learning the trade of carpentry. I wonder what creative work he built with a piece of wood, hammer and nails. Could it have resembled the rugged wooden cross he hung on? Where the nails he pounded in place like the ones that were hammered into his hands? How interesting that the connection to his earthly skill as a carpenter correlated to his destiny on the cross.

Look at your past skills and see if there is any talent you recognize you can use in your dream. Once you discover your God created purpose you will have a sense of passion and fulfillment.

It might not be a skill you connect with, but an experience that has made you somewhat of an expert in a particular area and now feel you can help someone else though that same place. Like myself, I learned a lot more medical knowledge of holistic health treatments through my health challenges. I also gained Spiritual insights as I pressed in with God and discovered new gifts. I have used these to inspire and help others grow in their knowledge of Spiritual principles to fight adverse times.

It may not be anything different than you're doing. Maybe you're in the right place of serving your purpose but you lack the opportunity to excel in your dream. Maybe you just need to develop your skill of endurance and resilience or self-confidence which we discuss in some of the other dream steps.

I pray you will discover and develop the skills you need to succeed in your destiny.

8

Network with Others-Discover Divine Connections
to Your Dream

"He called his twelve disciples to him."

~ MATTHEW 10:42 NIV

Although you don't like to promote yourself, you are your best promoter. You know what your plans and dreams are for your ministry better than anyone else. You know the details of how your dream can meet someone else's needs. Business cards are a great way to promote you! Use your creativity as to what you would like them to say. Passing them out is the best way to get your information into someone's hands. When the opportunity arises, you don't have to struggle looking for a pen and paper. Hand them out everywhere! Make a pamphlet or a flyer with your ministry information or bio. Newspaper columns, ads, special interest sections are other ways of making yourself known...Try placing your special screening's in the paper...many papers have a community section and it doesn't cost anything to place an add if it's for a not for profit organization. Contact the paper to do a story on your ministry!

I planned my own speaking engagement...twice! And I was successful at it. Contact local rotary clubs, lions clubs other associations where you might go do some speaking and invite people to your church. Let them know what your ministry has to offer. Put something on the net...get your own website. I'm still constructing mine.

Many local hospitals have monthly classes they offer the public. Contact their education department and let them know what unique topic you might bring...possibly a talk on overcoming grief, something on laughter being a good medicine...people need a good dose of laughter these day. Set up your own seminar...

Look for opportunities to Network and promote yourself. Networking is a way of learning from others and it makes you visible. "He who walks with wise men grows wise..." (Proverbs 13:10 NIV). Isolation can lead to a lack of motivation and be a dream destroyer. That's why another person with a similar passion and is a companion, "dream chaser" can propel you to move forward. "As iron sharpens iron, so one man sharpens another" (Proverbs 27:17 NIV). Hanging around others with similar visions helps fan the flame of our passions.

As a nurse manager I networked a lot and had other managers as friends and mentors. As a writer, speaker and coach I do the same. Others can be good examples to us.

Having relationships with other believers helps make us accountable. We all have blind spots. It's important to have someone point out to us when we are going in a wrong direction. We need to build a relationship with a special someone we can trust so that when they confront us with the truth delivered, in a loving way, we are open to receive it. This type of friend can help keep us in the center of God's will.

Keep searching for opportunities for someone who has expertise where you don't. Conferences, meetings, work environments, church groups or civic organizations can provide opportunities for you to network.

Here are some quick easy tips on what networking provides.

Helps you identify problems.

Gives you solutions and ways to handle them.

Can give you insights how to grow and expand in your career, relationships or finances. Books and magazines are great investments and the people who write them are helpful mentors.

Provides you with a mentor, who is someone that is successful at accomplishing a similar dream, and can impart valuable information to help you fill your desires.

In the Scriptures in Luke, chapter one, we are given the account of an angel coming to the Virgin Mary and informing her she has conceived a child. (This is the story of Jesus' miraculous conception). Earlier in the chapter, Mary's older relative, Elizabeth, also had a special angelic visitation where her husband and she conceived a child during their older years. After Mary's angelic visitation we are told she went to Judea to visit her relative Elizabeth. Elizabeth was already six months into her pregnancy. When I read this I pondered how God used Elizabeth as a mentor to Mary. She was already six months pregnant and could teach her some things about pregnancy and childbirth. She could also identify with her angel visitation. Could you imagine how perplexing that would be to others?

There was a special connection and mentoring going on between Mary and Elizabeth. It says, "Mary stayed with Elizabeth about three months and then returned home" (Luke 1:56 NIV).

There are many great examples of mentoring woven throughout the Bible. There was Moses and Joshua, Paul and Timothy, Queen Esther and Mordeci, her relative who helped her go from being a peasant girl to a palace queen.

The college I graduated from in nineteen-eighty-one recently held a networking event. Since it was in my neighborhood I decided to go. I thought I could help someone. In turn I got a lot of help myself. It was a very organized event. I made contacts with people that were willing to promote my speaking and encouraged others in their purpose as well. I explained to one man who had a dream to teach others, how to set up his own speaking engagements. I like to do an annual seminar on writing, publishing and speaking to mentor others with these aspirations.

Coaches are also great mentors as they help you motivate and keep your focus. They can help you live the life of your dreams

When I was a young girl the old cliché, *Birds of a feather flock together,* was popular. . A church congregation is sometimes referred to as a flock. I believe that's one of the reasons attending church is good for us. God wants believers to ignite each other's faith.

Hanging out with other people who are great believers of their dreams and achieve them are great motivators for you.

9

Discover Your Purpose and Succeed at Being Yourself - It's the Authenticity to Your Dream

"I cry out to God Most High,...who fulfills his purpose for me."

~Psalm 57:9

Before my call to write I felt there was something I was supposed to be doing that I wasn't aware of. *"I wish I knew what my gift is,"* I would say to my husband and good friend. They would ensure me I was a gifted nurse, and teacher as I taught childbirth classes and a Sunday school class, as well as many other patient education classes throughout my nursing career. Still I knew deep inside there was something more. So I started praying and asking God to show me what I was meant to do. Spending time alone in prayer and reflective listening led me to the surprising message to write.

When I discovered my new gift of writing it took some time to develop. I became aware of the fact we are all created for a special purpose. We possess potential, natural and spiritual talents and ability to succeed on our God-given life mission. However, many of us never see or reach that potential or use our gifts. We feel we're not worthy or valued by God. As you read this chapter, I encourage you to see yourself as unique and blessed on your mission!

If you're not sure of your purpose, read over the dream steps. They should help you determine God's plan for your life. When God was revealing a new purpose and gifts for my new season of life this Scripture was valuable in my pursuit of it.

"We all have different gifts, according to the grace given us. If a man's gift is prophesying, let him use it in proportion to his faith. If it is serving, let him serve; if it is teaching, let him teach; if it is encouraging, let him encourage; if it is contributing to the need of others, let him give generously; if it leadership, let him govern diligently; if it is mercy, let him do it cheerfully" (Romans 12:6-8 NIV).

Many people think having, "a call" on our lives is something exclusively given to missionaries, pastors or other church workers. Anytime we use our gifts and abilities to help someone else we are fulfilling our God-given call. During my many years of nursing, I was working on God's mission field of hospitals and clinics to heal and help others. One of the churches I attended had a wooden plaque above the door leading out of the sanctuary that read: *You are now entering the mission field.* The world is our mission field.

Our life is not like any other! We are all different, just as no two snowflakes are alike, each butterfly has its unique markings, and our fingerprints are all different. That's why fingerprints are a way to identify us! God has given us a unique identity. So why do we try so hard to be like someone else? When I was a teenager I bought all the popular teen magazines. I spent countless hours looking at the models and their perfect hair, skin and nails. I enjoyed the fashionable and flattering clothing they wore. Most of the time I felt like I fell short compared to these girls. I felt inferior because my skin had acne and bumps on it. At school I felt awkward because I was taller than any other girl or boy in my class. These issues in my life caused me to research how I could improve my flaws. I searched out the articles on how to care for your skin, hair and nails. I started applying them by working out a daily skin care routine to alleviate my acne. What I couldn't improve I covered up with techniques like the make-up artists used. I mixed and matched the few pieces of clothing I possessed to make a fashionable statement. When I noticed models were tall and thin like me, with the help of my parents, I went to modeling school. I discovered a few ways to like myself (improve my self-image), and use my unique qualities. Embracing our body type and characteristics helps us to become who God created us to be.

A friend of mine explained that for many years she had worked hard in the kitchen during church functions. She complained how one of the women she worked with was out in the front greeting the people and looking for attention, while she was slaving away in the kitchen behind the scenes. I explained to my friend it's possible this woman had a gift for hospitality and was acting as hostess at the event. I further explained when you go to a restaurant people are performing different functions; there is a busboy, waitress, hostess, kitchen help etc. Not all functions are as visible as the other, but each is extremely important.

About a week later my friend said she was enlightened. *"After all these years I have changed my attitude. I can't believe I never saw it that way before,"* she reported to me.

I enjoy learning about the various jobs others perform. I think how each one offers something to the world that wouldn't be possible without it. If we can see how our task fits in the scheme of things we can feel better about ourselves.

We are, "fearfully and wonderfully made" God explains in Psalm 139. We were designed to do some unique and amazing things. Learning more about ourselves and embracing who we are helps us become more confident.

I have listed a few points in this chapter to help you discover your unique qualities and embrace who you are!

Your personality traits play a unique part of your purpose. I learned about personality types in nursing school. We were taught this in our curriculum to help us understand and meet the needs of our patients. During my nursing career one of the hospitals I worked at had an employee health nurse who came to the clinic I managed. She gave a talk on personality types. Once the staff started learning more about their types they worked better and more efficient with each other.

During my greatest life/dream challenge God got my attention with this verse in Ephesians 3:16, "May He grant you out of the rich treasury of His glory to be strengthened *and* reinforced with mighty power in the inner man by the [Holy] Spirit [Himself in-dwelling your innermost being and personality]."

After reading this verse I realized God created our personality types. The ones we possess are an individual part of us that supports our gifts and purpose.

We have a great personality with traits specific to us. We might be a leader or a behind the scenes worker. We may have a personality that enjoys talking to people or playing music. We may be more compassionate and caring than another, and because of this we may enjoy working in a helping profession like counseling, teaching or nursing.

We may enjoy sports, or be more of the type that enjoys laughing and goofing around and become a comedian. Rather than our friend who tends to be a bit more serious and may be a teacher or leader.

We might have great organizational skills or have to work at this a little harder than our friend who is super- duper organizer! A peek in her closet reveals she has her clothes organized in a row according to their color.

There are complete books written on personality types. In her book Personality Plus, Florence Littauer, explains there are four distinct personality types: the Powerful Choleric, the Perfect Melancholy, the Peaceful Phlegmatic and the Popular Sanguine. I like to simplify them by describing them as Perfect, Peaceful, Popular and Powerful. That means for the most part your personality falls into one of these categories. Powerful people are usually leaders. Peaceful people normally tend to be peacemakers and peace keepers. Popular personalities enjoy being the life of the party and bring laughter with them. Perfect people desire to make the world a better place.

Once you know your personality type you can look at the characteristics you possess. Learning this information can help you have a better understanding of your emotional make-up and why you respond to life the way you do.

Look at your love language. As part of our unique personalities we have special "Love languages" (as explained by Dr. Gary Chapman in his book, The Five Love Languages). Some of us enjoy **giving** and receiving gifts as a token or expression of love. Others enjoy **acts of service.** We like it when someone does something for us or when we serve another. We may enjoy an **encouraging word** or embrace **a physical touch** such as hug or pat on the back from our friend or mate. **Quality time** can say, "I love you," like nothing else to a personality that needs some one-on-one with the one they love. Discovering someone's love language can improve the relationship between the two of you when you relate to them in the way that they receive love.

Considering your personal interests helps stop you from making unhealthy comparisons. We shouldn't compare ourselves with others. Their mission may be similar to ours. But each of us have a special blend of talents that are just right for us. The apostle Paul instructed us in 2 Corinthians 10:12 (KJV) "They that are comparing themselves are not wise." I find when I am starting to size up someone else to see how I compare to them, I say this little phrase, *"I will not compare or compete because in Christ I am created complete."* This means through believing in Jesus Christ, we have been created by God to complete a specific call and plan in this world.

Your hobbies and other interests are a part of your uniqueness as well. We should consider thinking about what we enjoy doing to pass the time. Maybe we like to exercise, read, cook, clean, or watch movies. Maybe we have gained a lot of expertise in these areas to help someone else. Those interests could become a career.

Your skills and gifts help you be your best. My mother and two older sisters had a gift for sewing. In my younger years I often admired the outfits they created. I decided if they could sew surely I could too. But try as I might, I couldn't get the hang of putting together patterns or the mechanics of keeping my thread untangled. One day I got the idea to save up for a special sewing machine like the one my oldest sister owned.

"Surely," I thought, *"With a top-notch sewing machine I could achieve my dream!"* The day came I got my machine. I kept it in the upstairs quarters where my parents-in-law lived. One day I went upstairs to set up my machine and start my journey as a seamstress. I searched all over the house to find my machine. It was gone... someone had taken it! No, I never found out where it disappeared. (But I had some suspicions). After that my desire to be a seamstress faded away. A short time later I went to nursing school. It was then I realized why I couldn't spend my time learning to sew. My time and talents were better spent on this design for my life.

Ask God to show you your unique attributes and add your unique spin to your life. In the love book of the Bible God declares, "...my perfect one, is unique" (Song of Songs 6:9 NIV).

Pay attention to the seasons of your life. Our timing may be different than someone with the same talents "My times are in your hands" (Psalm 31:5 NIV).

When waiting for a breakthrough or learning a new skill what takes someone else a few months, could be longer for us and vice versa. By competing with another's time frame we could get discouraged and give up. We must trust God's timing for us.

Listen to what your friends and others say about you. Do your friends compliment you or comment on things you are good at? If they are confirming what's in your heart this could lead to your purpose.

Embrace your life's experiences. What's the most important thing you've learned about yourself? Good or bad our troubles and trials can transform us to do something greater. When we learn things that take us through our painful experiences God uses what we have been through to help others go through. Scripture explains it this way, "Who comforts, (consoles and encourages) us in every trouble (calamity and affliction), so that we may also be able to comfort..." (2 Corinthians 1:4). Many a business, ministry or cause of some kind began this way.

Your Spiritual experiences shape your concepts of who God is and how you feel about Him. The things that tempt us are unique to us. Also our testimony in how we've come to know Christ is exclusive to us. Our life's lessons through failures, disappointments and the way Jesus trans-formed our life is valuable information to our purpose.

Open doors help discern your God-given direction. Paul identi-fied in 2 Corinthians 2:12 "The Lord opened a door for me there." I have found direction over the years through open doors. When I took a step of faith to become a nurse manager it was because out-of-the-blue my boss approached me about an opening for a manager on another unit. I'd never thought of being a manager or going into management. After prayerful consideration, I interviewed for, and accepted a posi-tion offered to me. This open door began my 10 year journey as a nurse manager.

Your age is a factor in your life. Moses was 80 years old when he led the Israelites out of Egypt into the Promised Land. At a recent speaker training conference I met an 83–year-old woman who was training to speak. I was amazed she was trying something new at her age.

The Bible mentions David was a young Shepard boy, when Samuel selected him as the upcoming king. Jesus' mother, Mary, was a teenager when the Holy Spirit used her to birth our Lord and Savior. Acts 2:17 declares "I will pour out my Spirit on all people. Your sons and daugh-ters will prophesy, your young men will see visions, your old men will dream dreams." This is proof that God uses young and old to fulfill His purpose.

Your education (whatever level it is), training and career experi-ence fulfills your purpose. I went to college but my sister didn't. However, she has had a successful career in the medical distribution industry. She has received on the job training and over-the-years she has advanced in her career into management as well as a teacher trainer. Her gifts are similar to mine, but they are developed and used in a different way.

Your disability is His ability. When my invisible disability with Environmental illness threatened to destroy my life, God showed me a plan and revealed that our disability is His ability to mold and shape our life. God revealed a new gift to me. I enjoy teaching how God uses our adversity and develops new hope and dreams in the midst of them if we seek Him. I have learned a lot about this disease and potential treatment modalities I didn't know before that benefit me as a nurse. I have also learned how to apply God's Word for healing and the power that prayer releases in the healing process. As a nurse I enjoy teaching others about Spirit, soul and body healing through my writing and speaking.

We don't need to stop dreaming because we have a disability of some kind. When I became housebound a friend gave me a book about Joni Eareckson Tada. Joni has a compelling life story. As a teenager she dove into a swimming pool and became paralyzed from the neck down. She struggled with why this happened to her. Over the years she learned how much God loves her. Through prayer and following the leading of the Holy Spirit she discovered amazing talents she possessed amidst her disabilities. To this day, she paints beautiful paintings while securing a paintbrush between her teeth. Positioned in her wheelchair she goes out and speaks to audiences world-wide revealing Christ's love. Her ministry

Your childhood play and experiences are like the puzzle pieces to your purpose. Sometimes are childhood dreams are illogical and unrealistic. We may desire to be an astronaut, and it may be a true dream or an elusive one. However, even if that is not what we were meant to be, we probably possesses some special qualities that would be necessary to become one.

Oftentimes, I look back at what my favorite childhood playtimes reveal. Among them, I enjoyed being a mother to my dolls. I also imagined I was taking their temperatures when they were sick, as a caring nurse. Other days, like a wise teacher, I lined up my dolls in front of my chalkboard and taught them the things I learned in school or Sunday school.

All these things from my past are like pieces of a puzzle put together that shape my life. Those pieces reveal my desire to be the wife, mother, nurse, teacher, writer and the Bible teacher I became. Take a look at your life and see if you can place some of the pieces to your life puzzle.

Through all your puzzle pieces God is preparing you for a specific purpose and a dream to be fulfilled. It states this in Ephesians 1:11

(NIV) when it says, "In him we were chosen, having been predestined according to the plan of him who works out everything in conformity to the purpose of his will."

10

Don't Allow Your Memories to Be Greater than Your Dream

"I do not consider myself yet to have taken hold of it. But one thing I do: Forgetting what is behind and straining toward what is ahead. I press on toward the goal to win the prize for which God has called me heavenward in Christ Jesus."

~ Philippians 3:13-14 NIV

I was beginning to live my dream of a being happily married. Jeff and I were establishing an apartment to move into as newlyweds. We would eventually get a house of our own, but things were happening fast and we were busy with wedding plans. There wasn't time to sell each of our homes and find a new one.

Then six weeks before the wedding, my house sold unexpectedly. I hadn't even placed it on the market! My oldest son's friend and his wife were house hunting. My son asked me, if I'd be interested in showing them the house... they decided to buy it and made me an offer I couldn't refuse.

This sale caused a lot of pressure, because I only had a few weeks to sort out and clean out my belongings and pack up the ones that I would take with me.

As I rummaged through every closet the decisions were hard as to what to let go of and what to take with.

This was where I lived for 18 years, while raising my family. The closets were overflowing with mementos that brought back a flood of memories; even the beat up broken toys, games, and clothing with rips, tears and stains the kids wore over the years, made my eyes gloss over with tears. *"When was the last time I cleaned out the closets?"* I whispered to myself, as the teardrops fell and I riffled my way through the menagerie.

When I completed the difficult task we stacked boxes, household items and furniture at the curb to discard for garbage pickup. When we were done I remember looking at the pile of my life's remnants and thinking what an enormous mountain it was.

The next morning, the first thing I did was go the window to see if the garbage had been picked up. I gasped at the transformed pile! Someone had lit a match to my stack of memories and all that remained was a mountain of gray ash!

After contacting the garbage collection company about what had occurred, I was instructed they would only remove the ashes if I had someone available to shovel them onto the truck.

I set up a collection day that Jeff would be available to help. I scheduled the truck to come during our lunch breaks. When the day arrived, I sat in my car waiting for about 15 minutes before the truck got there. My emotions were bitter-sweet as I had good feelings about moving forward and yet my soul ached with sadness at the departure of my old treasures and treasured memories surrounding them. When the truck arrived Jeff grabbed a shovel and began to pitch ash into the dumpster.

I watched in my rear-view mirror as my husband-to-be shoveled with all his might, the remains of my past. At that moment I felt a release from my painful past life. As I drove away, I changed my gaze from looking in my rear-view mirror to my front windshield with a larger view...you might say, I discovered a new point of view.

Not long after, I thought it was sort of whimsical when I heard an analogy about the rear-view mirror vs. the windshield in our car. Our rear-view mirror is small. It's designed to give us a glance of what's behind us. We use this for the purpose of discerning harmful traffic patterns coming up from behind or to back up on occasion. The mirror is small so it doesn't obstruct our view to see what's ahead of us.

This analogy is an example of how we're to view our lives. Sometimes a glimpse backward is okay in order to remember a special time we've had, learn something or remember an experience. For me it was the purpose of gaining some wisdom. When it comes to memories our lives should read like a history book- His Story- not like a prophecy of something to be repeated in our futures. And if it were to repeat we have the wisdom we've gained to get us through it. Most of life is to be lived looking ahead in the big window provided. If we persist in using our rear-view mirror while driving we'll never see what's up ahead and will crash and cause all sorts-of-problems.

The Biblical story of Lot's wife gives us a powerful depiction of a woman who was literally paralyzed and turned into a pillar of salt and crumbled because gazed with longing at her past, rather than moving forward into the plan God had in store for her. (Read this story in Genesis, chapter 19). Like her, we can become paralyzed and crumble our dream by continuing to focus on our past. We must look forward and move into our dreams. We can't allow those past memories to be greater than the God-given dreams that await us.

A few years later, I came across the Scripture passage that God will give us, "beauty instead of ashes" (Isaiah 61:3). The wind of His Holy Spirit blows away the ashes that are left over from Satan's attempt to destroy our dreams. This is God's promise to turn our past into something beautiful if we'll co-operate with Him and learn to let go of the old and embrace the new. As I read the passage I was amazed as I recalled the literal ashes of my past being shoveled away.

Many people never see the fulfillment of their dreams because they are stuck in the past. This activity can cause us to stay fearful, angry, unforgiving or remain unhealed from our hurts. Sometimes we can get stuck in memories of good things or accomplishments, the 'good old days' keep coming across our minds. We can feel fearful, discouraged or overwhelmed when thinking of our past. It can bring us images of regretful experiences and shame, rejection or hurt. I've experienced times such as these when I became housebound. I was in a season where things were changing and unfamiliar. Sometimes, I longed for the way things used to be in my life. As I focused on God I received new purpose and new ways to cope (which I am sharing throughout this book) and strength to move forward.

One of the great mysteries of our mighty God is that He can take our painful, tragic, and devastating past experiences and work them out for the good through the redirections in our lives. "And we know that in all things God works for the good of those who love him, who have been called according to his purpose" (Romans 8:28 NIV). I can't tell you how many times, I tearfully went to God and prayed that verse asking Him to work my trial out for good.

Although we don't want to allow our memories to become greater than our dreams, reminiscing from time to time can be a good thing. The famous philosopher Kierkegaard said, "Life can only be understood backwards." I like to say by connecting the dots of our lives we can find God's divine steps. Research proves there are healthy benefits to glancing at our past. We can recall life situations and integrate them into our present; doing this can help to develop meaning to our lives. We may see how God has worked things for our good. Reminiscing validates our life in a social and relational perspective; as we see the many friends, mentors and relatives who crossed our paths and shaped our lives. A walk down memory lane can increase our self-esteem and diminish feelings of isolation as we view the things we have overcome.

Taking a healthy look at the past can be good. But too much of a good thing can become dangerous when dwelling on the past, interferes with God's present plan. I know during my tough times I've had to be careful of not desiring to live in the past times that were better, but to use my past strengths to develop some forward movement. God instructs us to,"

Forget the former things; do not dwell on the past" (Isaiah 43:18). This doesn't mean he removes the former experiences from our memories; rather He has a way of making them not feel quite as painful as they were when the wounds to our hearts were fresh. But we must be patient in the process. I believe if we dwell too much on our past it's like dreaming backwards; thus, making our memories greater than our dreams.

Sometimes the toxic emotion of unforgiveness can hold us to our past. Each of us has found ourselves in some overwhelming circumstances challenging our ability to forgive. Sometimes, the other person isn't sorry for what they've done or they aren't here anymore. To forgive them sets our soul free. When we bear the grudge I've heard it's like ingesting poison and expecting the other person to die. In reality we only destroy ourselves! Scripture says that Satan gains an advantage over us when we choose not to forgive. Second Corinthians 2:11 warns us to forgive "in order that Satan might not outwit us. For we are not unaware if his schemes." Jesus instructed Peter to forgive, "seventy-seven times" (See Matthew 18:21-22). I believe this isn't an exact number but Jesus used this number because seven is the number of perfection; if we want to perfect our lives we'll have to forgive time and again.

Think of someone who you feel angry, hurt, or resentment towards. Tell God you choose to let go of those feelings toward them and ask for his help. Allow yourself time for the feelings to catch up.

If the problem is forgiving yourself, take a quiet moment and go deep into your place of self- resentment or regret. Take a deep breath and let it go. Envision it floating away like a helium balloon. Ask God to forgive you for this feeling and to help you love yourself in a balanced, not selfish, way. Tell yourself, "God loves me, I'm wonderfully made and I approve of myself."

Many people feel resentful toward God when life's disappointments hurt. Be aware of any resentment you have against God when life hasn't turned out the way you wanted it to. Allow yourself to offer back to God a prayer of gratitude, for the way He has shaped you. Make amends with God while you smile and hug yourself, thanking Him for the unique individual that you are at this exact place in time. In the Bible book of Esther, she went from peasant to Queen. The Scripture said she was born for such a time as this. So were you!

Thank God for the gift of forgiveness, obtained when Jesus died in your place. I've heard stories that people have been healed physically when they have forgiven someone. It physiologically changes our body chemistry and removes anger, resentment, depression, tension and releases healthy chemicals that promote healing.

Oftentimes, when we are hurt or betrayed we can feel victimized. When we are the victim of some wrong doing or hurtful circumstance we become powerful as we use our resilience to move toward restoring our life, rather than staying in a state of helplessness. In that place we have to look at what we can do differently to overcome our hurt.

Forgiving the person who hurt us is sometimes a process, but necessary for our well-being. Even though we have every right to be angry, we can get to a place of compassion toward that other person, understanding that there is something that has hurt them and they are functioning from an unhealthy place of hurt or misunderstanding and are not in a place where they need to be. If we stick to your core God-given values of love and forgiveness, we'll become the victor and not the victim. Ask God for His help to do this.

Forgiveness doesn't always mean reconciliation is possible. Sometimes the other person never changes nor desires to reconcile. Sometimes it's not safe or best to reconcile. Other times through open communication and mutual understanding trust can be rebuilt and reconciliation is possible. Each situation is unique. We have to decide how God is leading in your circumstance. The other person may never acknowledge their wrong doing due to their lack of spiritual insight. But we can move ahead and be free of harboring wrong feelings. I felt victimized by my health issues... besides that, there were people who didn't understand my issues and hurt me with their negative views and comments. I had to realize they just don't understand (how sad for them) that's why we are not to judge. Many times in our judgment wrong perceptions and lack of knowledge of a situation can cause us to misunderstand what the person is going through. We must make a wise judgment from a place of wisdom and understanding regarding each person's specific situation.

Place your focus on the person you want to be. That's how I became a writer, speaker and life coach. I used my lemons in life to make lemonade!

Once we experience a new beginning we will desire to share with others what God has done in our life! I once heard someone say, it's not that we forgive and forget; it's that we forgive even when we don't forget.

I pray this Scripture passage from Philippians 3:14 (NIV). "Forgetting what is behind and straining towards what is ahead." The apostle Paul revealed in this Scripture he doesn't mean he has lost all memory of his sinful or painful past, but placed it behind him, as he is done with it and settled with it. He doesn't allow it to get in his way he still strives toward that God given goal or dream.

11

Never Give Up! - Stay Committed to Your Dream

"Perseverance must finish its work."

~ JAMES 1:4 NIV

he worst thing is an unfulfilled dream. I've had dreams in my past that did not come to pass, but in hindsight I realized those dreams were not the ones God intended for me...they were something or someone I desired that wasn't God's best. In the long run I was much better off. Maybe you've dared to dream, followed all the steps and still wound up with a shattered dream. Maybe like me you were going down the wrong path. If your dream is broken it can be repaired or you can start over. If your dreams need to be rekindled cry out to God with your heart's desire; He can renew your dreams and heal your heart.

When we have a God-given dream we must guard it with all our heart. God instructs us in Proverbs 4:22 (NIV), "Above all else, guard your heart, for it is the wellspring of life." Time, circumstances, negative thinking of all sorts of things can come against us. It's our responsibility to keep our heart guarded against the negative thoughts and feelings that will cause us to give up.

One morning I remember being awakened out of a deep sleep with these words, *"These things take time, give it time."*

I think God was trying to get across to me time is an important dynamic in manifesting any dream. We're used to all the drive though conveniences of today's modern times. We see things in the present; God sees things in the BIG picture of eternity. We can't get concerned if we're not seeing the answers to our prayers in our timing. While we're waiting is a great time to spend a moment with God and become deeply acquainted with Him. Big dreams are birthed from spending big amounts of time in prayer and service. Allow God to bring you closer to Him.

Development takes time; whether it's building our character, a great relationship, a structure, or writing a book! Healing whether spiritual, mental, emotional or physical can take time (unless of course God provides a miracle, as I have seen and experienced Him do). So why do we think dream building is a quick and easy task?

Dreams help us overcome what looks impossible; they show us what God is possible of accomplishing in us, through us and for us. If God has given us a vision we must get excited about and work at it. Scriptures tell us that, "Faith without works is dead" (James 2:26 NIV).

Dreams and visions do not come to pass overnight, so we must stay dedicated to them even when we don't see any visual evidence indicating the fulfillment of them for a long time. "...In due time at the appointed season we shall reap, if we do not loosen and relax our courage and faint" (Galatians 6:9). Persistence pays off.

From the time of the discovery of our dream until it is finished, Satan comes to oppose our dream and plan. God has a plan for our lives, and so does the devil. He works through circumstances, people, our own emotions and excuses to get us to give up on our dreams and goals. He tempts us to compromise our thinking and leads us to believe that's the way to get to the fulfillment when in reality that results in an opposite outcome of misery, futility and emptiness.

He may tempt us to procrastinate though our weariness as time goes on. He's always got some tactic to try and hold us back from achieving God's best. If he can't get us to thwart God's plan altogether, he'll try to get us into some sort of adverse situation to set out to slow our progress.

Walking with God will bring obstacles. It's part of the price for pursuing a dream. The apostle Paul warns us that with every God-given opportunity comes some sort of opposition. "For a wide door of opportunity for effectual [service] has opened up to me [there, a great and promising one], and [there are] many adversaries." (1 Corinthians 16:9).

Remember it's been said that an optimist sees the opportunities in every obstacle and a pessimist sees an obstacle in every opportunity. Think of a time an obstacle may have become a new opportunity for you. It's a time to conquer our fears. If we can view our setbacks or obstacles as signs we're headed in a right direction we can stay persistent in moving forward.

All these reasons are why I believe God gave us the spirit of self-discipline so we could get moving and stay working on our dreams. Discipline and self-control are a fruit of the Spirit (Galatians 5:22) that God places inside of every believer. We have the choice to draw upon it. An example of this was I was sitting in my comfy chair for quite some time and knew I wanted to work on this book chapter. I prayed, God give me some energy and self-discipline to get me going. I made the decision to go into my office and I've been typing away ever since.

Using some self-discipline and standing against opposition can lead us to live a good life. God always works with us to fulfill His plan. So don't get discouraged or think it is impossible when the devil comes against you, God always has an alternate plan...

Ephesians 2:10 expresses, "For we are...recreated in Christ Jesus, [born anew] that we may do those good works which God predestined (planned beforehand) for us [taking paths which He prepared ahead of time], that we should walk in them [living the good life He prearranged and made ready for us to live]."

God planned a destiny for our good. As believers in Christ we receive His good plan when we believe Jesus died for our sins. Then as we learn to listen and allow Him to lead and guide us, throughout our life He will show us through Scripture verses and specific instructions through our Spiritual insight and intuition on how to carry out the plan.

God doesn't love us any more or less regarding whether or not we fulfill His plan, but our lives will be better if we do.

When I realized God was leading me to go outside because some of the elements that were a problem in my past were no longer an issue, I decided to make a plan to keep going out so they wouldn't be a problem again.

I adapted the mindset that I was not going to be housebound anymore and I decided to not give up! (As Christians we are called to be faithful to our calling and not give up. The men and women of the Bible suffered great hardships but keep going none-the-less.)

No matter what the weather I kept up my plan to go outside. When weather was too cold, hot, rainy or snowing I would go for just a few minutes, sometimes I'd just go to the end of my driveway and retrieve the daily mail delivery from our mailbox. Otherwise, I dressed for the occasion either in attire that was cool or warm depending on the weather and went out for a daily walk. I started five minutes a day, then twenty, then more! It's still a challenge in the extreme cold or hot weather, however. But I believe to overcome that too, or to go regardless of my symptoms.

One day late winter, I was walking on my patio. It was still very cold and damp outside. I stayed behind the house to block the winds from chilling me. I walked back and forth comfortably bundled in my hat, scarf and coat to keep warm while I took my afternoon walk.

I glanced down on my patio and noticed a teeny-tiny creature walking with me. I bent down for a closer glance, the small black spots on her wings and her oval shape and minuscule size made me notice I was being accompanied by a lady bug. She was walking ever-so-slowly and a closer look revealed she had icicles on her wings!

Oh, little lady bug, I thought to myself, *what a tenacious spirit you have. You're out here fighting these elements, and determined to survive just like me!*

I felt like she replied the Scripture verse in Philippians 4:13, *I can do everything through him who gives me strength.*

This little bug reminded me of the ant. In the Proverbs we are told the ant is persevering. With the ant in mind, my friend and I would sing the song, "High Hopes." I like to include that song whenever I speak on the subject of hope. Hope makes our hearts lighter and brings a smile to our face. My friend, Betty King said, "While watching the tiny ant drag food, it's not the size of the object that matters, but the perseverance that brings it victory!"

When writing this chapter I did a spell check on the word persistent; it came up as persist ant. I thought that was amazing! To me this was God's way of saying persist like the ant.

We can make some progress even when we feel like we're just going through the motions. If we do our part God will bring the results.

We must keep our hope high and never give up on our dreams! Hope is the spiritual force along with our faith that will keep us fighting for our dream. I discovered some wonderful Bible passages on hope that kept me hopeful. We've all felt the emotions in this Scripture verse at one time or another, "Hope deferred makes the heart sick, but a longing fulfilled is a tree of life" (Proverbs 13:12 NIV). Deferred hope is feeling hopeless. When we defer something we are essentially pushing it aside. But staying hopeful bring a tree of life. A tree of life is healthy and green giving off oxygen and life to those within its proximity. When our dreams come to pass we feel alive, elated, healthy and vibrant and are able to be a blessing dispensing good to help someone else have a better life. Remaining hopeful helps us to persevere.

"May the God of hope fill you with all joy and peace as you trust in him, so that you may overflow with hope by the power of the Holy Spirit." Faith is not about being hopeful of what we see happening to us. It's about placing our hope in God. Our God is one of hope. He desires us to be hopeful not hopeless. If we hold on to hope and refuse to give up we will see our dreams come true!

12

Be a Risk Taker and Step into Your Dream

"If you wait for perfect conditions, you will never get anything done."

~ Ecclesiastes 11:4 (TLB)

I've often heard it said that many people die with their dreams inside of them. I had a friend that told me a story about her friend who had a strong desire to write and was a very gifted writer. However, she never took the risk to get herself published. She died without ever publishing one thing. That story encourages me as a writer to keep working at it. God has filled us with great talents, skills and abilities and dreams to be fulfilled. If we have a vision for our life we're going to have to take a chance at achieving it some time or another.

I've heard many writers say they can't stand the thought of rejection, so they don't take a risk and submit a writing anywhere. They can sit and think about it every day of their life, but by doing so, they won't live out God's marvelous plan.

Our comfort zone gets in the way of achieving a better way of life. We can't achieve a dream while holding on to a limitation of some kind. If our dreams are easy for us to achieve, then chances are, they are not a big God-given dream. God given dreams take risks to achieve them. Since my childhood my older sister Lea would say. "Nothing ventured nothing gained." That's what risk taking is all about. She was good at bring up quips and quotes about life.

We need to identify our comfort zone. Our comfort zone may be an addiction to something, such as alcohol, medications, food, work, or someone (due to the constant need other people's approval). When we have trouble confronting or standing up to our issue, because of unknown fears, it's an indication we're afraid to shake and shatter our comfortable world as we know it.

The problem with coming out of our comfort zone is it can be difficult and emotionally challenging. There are great obstacles to overcome. We don't have to minimize the emotional pain, but to overcome we can't allow our fears to amplify it.

Sometimes we have to take a big risk to discover and fulfill a BIG dream. Oftentimes, we're waiting for conditions to be right. Planning is good within reason. Having a plan and preparing is wise and necessary, however, after careful and wise planning and preparation it's times to take a leap of faith. We have to put some action behind that plan. If we hold on to and only do what is comfortable we're not dreaming BIG enough! We have to stretch beyond our zone of comfort. "Stretch your curtains wide" (Isaiah 54:2 NIV).

We can't throw caution to the wind, however. I've heard Nik Wallenda, the famous tightrope walker, explain how he plans and practices his walks and the elements that could be a problem for him before he takes the risk. He prays as well and keeps his focus on what he is doing. He goes forward to perform after great prayer and preparation knowing God has called him to take the step. "According to the plan shown you" Exodus 26:30 (NIV).

A few of my big risks include approaching publishers and editors to take a risk on my writings. Remember, faith overcomes a lack of skill, education, or preparation. Other times, faith connects with your skill.

Taking bold steps to confront an issue with another person has been something I've had to work on over the years. And the *greatest* step I've had to take has been fighting my fears and trying new supplements or medications because I've had tremendous sensitivities, causing frightening symptoms when taking them. Going out of my house after eight years of trying and failing a multitude of times was a knee-knocking step of faith.

Major efforts to take a step of faith included looking at my failures and my feelings of fear regarding trying supplements and reaching inside for the God-given courage within that I didn't realize I possessed to do what He was asking me to do to try things and step out in faith when the time was right. God gives each of us the courage to do what we've been called to do-even when we don't feel we have any. It's when we stretch ourselves in spite of our feeling afraid we are using courage. If we want to embark on a future bigger and brighter than where we are, we must overcome our fear with risk taking faith. Also remember we don't have to be perfect, just do things as excellent as possible and let the rest go.

I found encouragement in one of my favorite Bible accounts regarding risk taking. The disciple, Peter, saw Jesus walking on the water. Peter was adventurous and bold at times. He felt Jesus was inviting him to come and join Him, "Lord, if it is You, command me to come to You on the water" (Matthew 14:28), he called out.

When we know the Lord is commanding us to do something it always involves a risk of faith to fulfill. Peter took the steps to meet Jesus on the lake. However, his faith got shaky and he failed. But he got further than the other eleven disciples that stayed in the boat. And besides, Jesus came to his rescue! (When our attempts at faith fail, Jesus will help us back up!).

I knew God had some greater things for me to achieve but I couldn't do them without getting out of my house (my boat so to speak).

When it was time for me to try going out of my house after eight years, I had to do it afraid. I didn't know what type of symptoms I might encounter, but I felt like God was pushing me to get moving forward. I found a new life awaited me. And I didn't encounter some of the problems with car exhaust I once did. But, I didn't know that ahead of time, it wasn't easy taking that risk to find out.

We may wonder what our boat is. It's a place of comfort and ease that holds us back from something better for our life. Most people hold back like the other eleven disciples and never live a fulfilled life.

We become stronger in our faith when we do the thing we were once of afraid of. The world has a cliché that goes something like this: "Fake it until you make it!" However, I think as believers we are to stay strong in our faith and "faith it until we make it!"

"Now, faith is being sure of what we hope for and certain of what we do not see" (Hebrews 11:1 NIV).

We don't have to know everything or have it all figured out before taking a step of faith. Fulfilling the dream will be a process of learning, growing, developing, trying and failing. I shared this Scripture verse with a man I was coaching and it changed his perspective on taking a risk. "Though a righteous man falls seven times, he rises again" (Proverbs 24:16 NIV).

I enjoy reading true life stories about men and woman who tried and failed their way to success. In fifth grade I read a story about a woman who as an infant battled a fever that left her blind, deaf and dumb. Years later, a woman entered her life and worked miracles helping her to read, write and communicate with others. The woman was Helen Keller and her miracle worker's name was, Ann Sullivan. Ann was an example to Helen of a risk taker since Helen's parents were, oftentimes, at odds with Ann. But eventually Ann's ability to take risks to stand up to Helen's parents allowed her to help Helen. In turn, Helen became a risk-taker herself. Helen was a Christian who went on to write many books, stories, and articles encouraging others to take risks and fight the odds against them. Think about whom might benefit from our risk taking steps to achieve our BIG dream.

Remember our dream will cost something. Jesus told us in Luke 14:28. "Suppose one of you wants to build a tower. Will he not see if he has enough money to complete it?" When something costs us we need to make an investment whether the investment is spiritual, emotional or financial wealth; we need to look at what the cost is and examine if we're willing to invest what it takes. Bringing a dream to pass costs time, money, and emotional challenges. We need to be willing to take risks in all of these areas. Reading books and attending seminars or researching what it costs to build our dream, is part of spending time on the risk-taking process.

I've heard it said that taking a risky step toward our dream is going from the mindset of "What if" that holds us back, to the present state of "What is" where our dream is reached or realized.

If we're not sure where to begin, we can start with small steps. I went outside for five minutes each day and worked my way up. Small steps can lead to BIG dreams! Just remember to take those steps. If we feel we don't have enough confidence to take that risk, we can take a deep breath and know that every step in this book is how to grow our confidence. If we implement the steps we will build up our confidence. One of the greatest analogies I use to move forward is remembering the old adage, "How do you eat an elephant? One bite at a time." Or one small step at a time.

If we want an abundant life we have to take the risk to discover and enter into it; like the four lepers mentioned in 2 Kings 7:4, who were sitting in a city that was in a famine. One day they realized that the only way they could survive was by taking the chance to go to a nearby city. However, they weren't sure how safe that strategy was, because the Syrian army there may kill them. They said, "Why sit here until we die?" They knew if they stayed where they were they would die for sure, so they took the risk and God protected them.

Many aspects of our lives require taking risks. When we have been hurt we have to take the risk to forgive. When someone has betrayed us, it can be difficult to trust again. Even though we need to use good discernment when to trust, and not throw caution to the wind, we can't become cynical and untrusting, either. We must learn to trust again. It's a risk we have to take. We can always trust God to lead us and guide us.

We can't allow our obstacles to hold us back always finding another excuse to keep from moving ahead. When we hear the Spirit leading, with God's help, we can be cool, calm, calculated and confident to take our risk.

13

Enjoy Where You Are On the Way to Where You Are Going and Watch Your Dream Unfold

"The thief comes only in order to steal and kill and destroy. I came that they may have and enjoy life, and have it in abundance [to the full, till it overflows]."

~ JOHN 10:10

As I write this today, I wonder where you're at in the progress of fulfilling your dreams. One of my greatest dreams is to achieve the promise in this Scripture verse, to have and enjoy life that is filled with abundance. My granddaughter recently asked me what "abundant" means. One explanation of abundant means, "plentiful". My personal explanation of a plentiful life is it is a life that involves amazing favor, spiritual insight and understanding. It also includes a confident spirit, great personal satisfaction, a calm and peaceful thought life, vibrant physical health, wonderful friends that bring out the best in us, meaningful work that fulfills our purpose and provides plentiful provision. A loving family that overflows with joy and compassion would also be included!

Last night before I went to bed I was thinking about the many things that were concerning my mind. Health issues came up, as well as some financial constraints. I had been sick with a cough besides other chronic health issues; God is faithful to answer the prayer for healing and I am feeling better today. It's Christmas and an expected expense came up that threatens my Christmas budget- and that can quench the Christmas Spirit. But, I decided not to allow the devil to steal my Christmas joy! It's my choice, after all. When I woke up this morning I started singing Christmas carols. I'm also enjoying writing to you.

It seems everything good in life takes work. You've heard the old saying, "no pain no gain" even enjoying each day is something we have to go through the pain of working at!

Wherever we are on life's journey it isn't going to do us much good if we're miserable while trying to arrive at our destination. We need to enjoy the trip as well. Sometimes, I wonder if we'd learn to enjoy our trip more we might have quicker and easier arrivals and BIGGER dreams imparted to us! Enjoying where we are on the way to where we're going is about regaining our joy before our dream is complete.

There's nothing like a dream vacation, an unexpected surprise or a bonus on our paycheck to bring us joy. Like the rest of the world, these things excite me! But what about all the mundane days that occur between that vacations and special days. How do we enjoy them?

My sister gave me a cup that says, "Celebrate Life" on it. I like that motto. I think it's one we should all try to achieve. I found in my hard places of being housebound and overcoming loss I could learn to choose to enjoy my life. I think we make finding the enjoyment in life complex, and that's why we don't enjoy it. Everyday isn't a party or payday, but we can make it a good day even if it's not our best day. If we look at the small things and learn to enjoy them, each day becomes a celebration of life.

When we become a Christian it's not just about receiving eternal life, but about a new way to live in this life, and a different way of handling problems through changing perspectives. If our perspective is positive it can open up amazing possibilities, but if it's negative we can have depression and lack.

God didn't intend us to separate our ordinary daily tasks of daily living from our spiritual life. Actually, our spiritual life should help us carry out our ordinary daily tasks with joy. When we pray daily it shouldn't be a burden but an invitation for God to help us through our day. We can enjoy work knowing God is with us and is fulfilling our purpose in some way and leading to that big dream! We can be kind to others around us and practice living out the Christian principles of love each day. We do our jobs with excellence and enjoy that we did our best, even if it isn't the best job or the best day at our job.

Our work can be a way to help others. My friend is going on a mission trip to another country. That sounds so exciting to me. I used to desire to go on a mission trip. As a young wife and mother, I couldn't leave my family responsibilities to go. I found if we can't go when we can give to others who can it is like we're going. Later in my life God showed me that my work was my mission field. I was on the mission field helping in each hospital I worked at. I was on the mission field of my home as a wife and mother. And now, I am on the mission field of writing, and speaking to help others fulfill their God-given dreams.

Helping others is a way of serving God. Our dream should involve making a difference in others' lives. Besides, blessing others has a way of bringing blessing back to us. Jesus said, "Give and it shall be given unto you."

Plan activities to do each day that will produce joy; when I was housebound I looked at the little things I could enjoy. A phone conversation with a friend; a good movie; an interesting book or CD to teach me new things were life's incidentals I found enjoyable. I wrote, and volunteered to lead our church's phone prayer chain, and I did some teaching by phone through Tele-seminars. I stopped complaining about how I felt all the time and started focusing on what I could do to bloom where I was planted for the time being. (I realized complaining only made me feel more miserable). When we constantly complain we remain unchanged. I realized the people around me didn't want to hear me complaining all the time. That doesn't mean we can never discuss how we feel. There is a reality to the situation. However, if we overdo it, we start feeling miserable.

I had other days when I just sat and looked out the window and dreamt of feeling better and being out in the world again. I figured that was the best I could do to enjoy that day. We need days of rest, too. Resting can be a time to dream. Dreaming BIG is a way to take us from the mundane common life into something beyond what we can imagine and only God can fulfill. Dreaming BIG takes us into another dimension beyond who, what and where we are, to who and what we can become at another time. It can help us enjoy ourselves better, knowing God has *"a hope and a future"* for us (Jeremiah 29:11 NIV). Dreaming invites a bigger better future into our life.

Have you ever considered enjoying right where you are? I know, I've been in some pretty un-enjoyable circumstances. That's why joy has to be worked at. Problems will come and go in our lives. We can use them to become better or bitter. God's uses problems to test our emotional stability.

Have you ever pondered what is taking your joy away? I realized several years ago, most of our problems focus around finance, health and relational issues. Then, there's our spiritual life which many times we feel bad about because we think we're not good enough for God to love us, or out of ignorance, we just don't believe God.

Let's look at a few of the "little foxes" (I think of them as the detours) spoiling our dream to enjoy life. The reason I mentioned little foxes is because foxes are sly, crafty and deceptive, like these emotional deceptions we're discussing. Early one Sunday morning, I looked out the kitchen window and noticed two red foxes in my back yard. There was one on each side of the grandkids swing set standing there like pair of bookends. Within a day or so, while reading my Bible I came across a Scripture that caught my attention because of those little foxes. The verse read: "Catch for us the foxes, little foxes that spoil the vineyards" (Song of Solomon 2:15).

I asked God to show me what this meant. Since that day, I have learned these are those little deceptions in life that spoil our vine of joy-the connection we have between us and God. They are sly as a fox, because they often go unnoticed by us. Self-pity, depression, worry, criticizing, complaining, excessive thinking trying to figure things out, are just a few that block our view of peace or joy.

There's a lot that can be said about enjoying where we are. Books are written on how to enjoy life. Since I only have a few pages left in this book, I'll briefly mention a few things that helped me.

Embrace each moment. Several years ago, I heard a woman mention she disciplined herself to enjoy each task she did no matter how mundane it was. She said eventually new and exciting things started coming her way. She attributed this to the fact she focused on getting the most of enjoying each day.

Also, identity activities that could be "dream wasters." They drain us of energy and are considered idle time. They don't count as a "dream builder" because they don't attribute to a positive lifestyle. Too many hours on mindless T.V. can cause us to get distracted and take whittle away the precious hours that could be used in preparing or pursing the building our dream.

God gave us entertainment. We can watch T.V. read a book, play a game or listen to a song, or play with a child. We don't have to go to the gym to exercise, we can take a walk, and I've enjoyed walking since my childhood and still do. We can enjoy the view along the way. We can take a nap or rest (these are some of the things I mentioned I did and still do!).

Simple choices make or break our joy. A choice to be happy or sad, or worry excessively; or to spend money on something we can't afford but we desire. Yet, once and a while we need to treat ourselves. Being doubled-minded will frustrate our enjoyment as we try to struggle with a decision about what is the right thing to do (I dealt with this over many decisions and the issue of trying to figure out how I could get out of my house). Now just going to the store to buy a product can be a major decision in what to buy. Multi-tasking can be an asset but it can also leave us feeling overwhelmed if we take on too many tasks. As a nurse I had multiple patients relying on me at one time. I had to do many things at once. It can be stressful. Being in a hurry will zap our ability to "stop and smell the roses," otherwise, meaning our ability to see the positive beauty of each day. A friend of mine used to say, Remember today is the present because it's God's gift to us, so keep it simple.

Most people probably don't reach the fulfillment of their dreams because they either don't understand what I'm explaining right now, have never been made aware of this principle, but keep doing the same thing that makes them miserable. The apostle Paul gave the same instruction to the Corinthians. They must have been complicating their lives as well. His message to them was, "But I fear, lest somehow, as the serpent deceived Eve by this craftiness, so your minds may be corrupted from the simplicity that is in Christ (2 Corinthians 11:3 NKJV). He is saying Satan tries to complicate things.

Dread can take the joy out of the present moment. I noticed I had dread facing another day of sensitive reactions to food and things in my environment. It made me not want to face another day. Instead, I learned to focus on what I had left in my life to motivate me. Sometimes we dread things such as going to work (especially on Mondays), doing a specific household chore such as dishes or some other task. Dread can cause us to procrastinate. Procrastination is a joy thief because it causes us to put things off, and we will either miss an opportunity and later on regret that we put it off. Regret then takes over and steals more joy because it holds us in the thought pattern of the past when we think, "if only" I had done this. Do any of these things sound familiar to you?

When I was a young girl I learned to do the tasks I dreaded first. I liked to get my homework out of the way so I could enjoy the rest of the day. Now, I am learning this is still a good approach to tackling an unpleasant project; but sometimes I find I need a whole new perspective on the task so I can learn to like it.

Too much responsibility causes stress. Taking on tasks that aren't ours to do, can burden us with things that aren't our responsibility; then we feel overwhelmed. Delegating the things we can to others, such as having the kids help with chores or handing out jobs to others they are capable of accomplishing can help us be more relaxed. Doing this is a part of establishing healthy boundaries. Healthy boundaries prevent 'burn out" feelings of exhaustion from struggling with things too hard for us to handle on our own. Learning to say yes when asked to do a favor when our heart really means yes, or no when you really don't think you can fit it in our schedule or don't have the ability to do is setting a good healthy boundary. We tend to say yes, instead of no to many things we really don't feel led to do. Then we overextend ourselves and feel resentful causing hurt, pain and needless anguish.

Enjoying where we are doesn't mean we stay stuck where we are or diminish our dreams to get there...it's to look at our progress and enjoy the work we're doing today, and believe somehow it will help us achieve our dreams. Look at every little step of the way as joyful.

Patience is part of the journey. Just like the map at the mall or on your G.P.S. (I've heard it called our God Positioning System) getting to your destination takes discovering the way there and time to get there. While God is working to move us forward things need to take place in order for us to get there, patience is necessary to enjoying our journey to the promised land, "For you have need of steadfast patience *and* endurance, so that you may perform *and* fully accomplish the will of God, and thus receive *and* carry away (and enjoy to the full) what is promised" (Hebrews 10:36). Without patience we won't see the fulfillment of what we are waiting for. If we get impatient we may take a different direction than God's plan. God is testing our faith during that time and it's only by enduring the wait that we will have the joy of a fulfilled dream. Patience doesn't mean we have the answers either; sometimes we have to wait patiently for those as well. In the meantime, we can take a deep breath or sigh of relief. As a childbirth educator I understand the importance of taking a deep breathe. A deep breathe or sigh of relief oxygenates our brain and every organ in our bodies. It can relieve physical pain. It can clear our head so to speak, and calm our nerves. When we find ourselves anxious in God's waiting room, stop and take a deep breathe. Ask the Holy Spirit which Scripture refers to as the "breathe of life" to fill us. We don't want to make hasty choices that can cause setbacks or complicate our situation. When anxiety arises... take a breath or pause

When I first started writing, I came across this passage, "Begin the joyous tasks I have assigned to you" (Matthew 25:21 LB). I realized when we are fulfilling our God-given dreams the tasks of work as well as play are to be enjoyed.

Enjoying where we are is about listening to our inner life. What is God saying to us? What are our own thoughts and emotions directing us to think, and feel like today? We can change our minds to enjoy what we are doing even if it's not exactly where we desire to be. We can create a new atmosphere around us when we set a goal to enjoy our life. Enjoying each day begins with changing our thoughts and perceptions about our day.

While housebound I hung up some wall hangings with the saying, "Live, Laugh and Love." These are the way to achieve enjoyment. Live with Godly values; Love in big and small ways each day. Saying "I love you" is important to build healthy relationships; laugh often. I heard a doctor say we should laugh at least 10 times a day, to balance out our stress." If we're not a person who knows how to laugh, hang with a friend who does laugh often. The laughter can be contagious.

While we're on the journey not everything we face is going to bring joy. But we can't always see what's going on in the Spirit realm. God could be ready to bring a break through or promote us to the next step at any time. We must be determined not to allow the devil to steal our joy as we make progress to enjoy where we are.

14

Health and Beauty - The Physical Fitness to Your Dream

"You were bought with a price (purchased with preciousness and paid for, made his own). So then, honor God and bring glory to Him in your body."

~ I CORINTHIANS 6:20

You're making good progress with your steps; but as a nurse and one who is striving to become physically fit for her journey, I feel I can't come to a close without giving you a few simple tips to optimal health so you'll have the physical fitness and stamina to fulfill your dream.

Through my own journey with illness the one thing I have learned is how important taking care of ourselves in the area of our physical health is. Without it we can't be productive in reaching our dream, or have great relationships with God or others. When we don't feel our best we are tired and don't have energy to do what we need to. It took me over six years to get this book written as I paced myself because I'm still challenged with some health limitations but try to work with what I can do.

I enjoy the fact that in the "Our Father" prayer, one of the verses Jesus taught us was "Your Kingdom come Your will be done, On earth as it is in heaven (Matthew 6:10). One of the things I realized is that there are no diseases or health issues of any kind in heaven. We just need to believe for the promise this prayer provides to manifest in our lives.

How we take care of ourselves physically affects our spiritual and mental emotional well-being. If we are tired or sick it can affect our spiritual life, because we won't feel like praying. Emotionally we can become cranky and irritable instead of the loving, kind individuals God desires us to be. We can get easily discouraged when we are tired or ill. The better we feel physically the more confident we feel toward pursing our dreams.

Learn to listen to your body, God made us so wonderful that our body will send us cues regarding our basic needs. If you get in tuned to it, you'll discover what you need to do in specific situation. A nurse friend of mine impresses this with patients all the time. I've had times when a doctor's recommendation didn't feel right to me, so I didn't proceed with it. They aren't always right either. That's why you need to pray and follow how God is leading you. Your intuition regarding your health problem matters and is an important key to solving the problem. Remember you are the boss of you! Simply put, if you feel thirsty you will drink. If you're tired you'll nap or get some extra rest. You may notice subtle food allergies after you eat something. Noticing you feel, tired, foggy headed, muscle stiffness or emotionally irritable can be a possible indication of sensitivity to something. Other times, it may be you've gotten extreme by taking too much of a good thing.

As a nurse I'm blessed with education and knowledge about health, which gives me a special discernment toward understanding health treatments. However, I think reading, listening to the health shows on radio or T.V. can provide you with basic knowledge you need. You'll be surprised what you can pick up about your health and healthy solutions. I've learned things I never learned in nursing school or on the job by reading books, articles or listening to health topics. I recommend listening to one health program or reading one health related article a week. This can increase the knowledge you need to take care of your bodies.

Here are some simple health habits:

Exercise: There are two factors regarding age; one is your chronological age which is the number of years you've lived on earth, the other is your physiological age, the age your body appears like. You can be 60 but have the physiological health of a 50 year-old if you keep yourself in shape. One of the ways to do this is with exercise. Just by incorporating a little movement into your day you can keep your muscles and joints from becoming stiff and achy. I know there are times this isn't possible but even if you move your fingers you're still moving a joint and keeping an area limber. When I was housebound I walked several times a day inside my home. While working at the computer I make sure I get up each hour and take a break.

If you're not what you'd call an avid exerciser start with the basics. If you can walk, you have a special blessing. My friend has had a debilitating back issue and desires to walk, but is unable to. I have been challenged by Fibromyalgia stiffness in my feet and have endured foot pain in the past. But I have worked through and around some of my issues to sustain my ability to walk. I've always enjoyed walking. It started in my childhood when I had to walk to school. I know you've heard the old story, "I walked a mile to school." I walked down the hill. Then I had to walk back up the hill. The going down part wasn't so bad, but going against the gravity uphill took some energy. As the years progressed, I became a teenager and did have to walk a mile to school. I also had friends on the other side of town whose house I walked to on a regular basis, since my mother didn't drive and my father worked all day. I learned my feet were a good source of transportation.

I've learned since to enjoy a leisurely stroll through the neighborhood or local walking trail. Looking at the sights can relax your senses while your body motion keeps you moving forward. I remember enjoying the variety of colorful flowers others planted. Walking past the pond I could hear the frogs croaking and see one occasionally leap past me. Even a red-headed woodpecker wearing his God-given tuxedo could be seen flying from a near-by treetop.

When I was housebound I would walk around the house. Each day I would spend fifteen to twenty minutes walking in place or back and forth in my living room and kitchen. Now, there's times I walk in my driveway, or go to the mall to avoid the extreme heat or cold to keep up my walking routine.

You might schedule in a brief 20 minutes and enjoy a brisk walk in the park. You can also use some of these tips I've done over the years, such as making sure you use the stairs when possible, park at the far end of the lot, or step in place. Some of the video games with activities such as bowling or golf can be a fun way to get in a few moments of exercise. Just remember start slow and gently increase. Walking with a friend can make it an enjoyable time.

Housework is a great source of exercise. While vacuuming I remind myself I am utilizing my time wisely, stretching my muscles and my stamina while obtaining a clean house! You can GOOGLE how many calories you burn while performing a particular household task.

Hydration: Drink plenty of water. The world consists of two-thirds water and so do our bodies. I learned the benefits of water in my early teens. I went to modeling school at the age 13. I never became a model but learned many valuable health and beauty tips that I still use today. One of them was to drink lots of water. It provides energy and prevents wrinkles!

I was plagued with acne. It was all over my cheeks. No matter what soap, cleansing cream, astringent, or ointment I tried (and believe me there were many!) I still got breakouts. I learned drinking water would help hydrate my skin, keep it looking younger, and flush away impurities that could cause toxins in my bloodstream contributing to breakouts of acne. With that information I started training myself to drink several glasses a day. It's recommended to drink at least 8-8oz glasses of water each day.

(Unless you have a health issue and your doctor has a restriction on how much fluid you consume each day). I started by drinking a glass before I went anywhere, and anytime I was thirsty I grabbed water. Now I drink about half of my water consumption between the time I wake up and lunchtime. This is because I haven't had water all night. And it refreshes me in the morning hours. Then I drink the rest throughout the course of the day. Sometimes I break it up into thirds, I drink one-third in the morning, afternoon and evening. Remember when you are working in hot weather and sweating excessively, you may need to increase your water consumption. This applies if you have a fever as well. Sometimes, I watch my water consumption toward evening. If I drink too much in the later hours of the day that means excessive trips to the bathroom that night, breaking up my sleep.

You don't have to increase your new habit of drinking water all at once...start a little at a time. Drink a glass here and there, or start with half, even a few sips is better than nothing! If water is taken from your faucet it is better if you can place a filter to decrease chlorine and other chemicals that purify it, or a bottled water will do; you can try several different brands to see what tastes best. Believe or not, all water doesn't all taste the same. Some people add a squeeze of lemon for some flavor.

As a nurse other greats benefits I've learned about water is it can help organs function well as it lubricates and keep them moist, rids our body of toxins that are stored in muscles, tissues and important organs such as the brain and liver. It can sharpen our thinking process! It aids in maintaining adequate blood volume since two thirds of our bodies is water. The plasma portion of our blood is water. (It transports nutrients through the body, increases our metabolism which is a great help for weight loss, forces fat to be used as fuel and contains no calories! That is a beneficial beauty tip!).

You won't live long without proper hydration. As a nurse I hung Intravenous fluids on countless number of patients. Adequate hydration helps fight infection and decrease fever. Ingesting the right amount of water each day can improve your energy level and overall well-being.

Drinking too many cola drinks or coffee (because they contain caffeine) or alcohol beverages can dehydrate your body. Drink a glass of water and you'll feel refreshed!

Detoxify: We all have a toxic buildup in our bodies. I've learned on my health journey that this can be the root of many illnesses. One of my jobs as a nurse was to make sure the environment complied with the standards for eliminating wastes. We discarded old medications, which are chemicals, in a special way using bio hazard boxes and labeled as bio hazard materials.

Our modern day environment is filled with potentials hazards. We have pesticides and herbicides (which keep the pests out of our gardens), and powerful petrochemicals, (you see these on the oil spills).

Agriculture has inundated our foods with Hormones and antibiotics that are damaging the nutritional quality of the foods we eat. (This can be remedied by the taking daily requirements of nutritional supplements).

Toxins invade the air we breathe. I've invested in an air purifier in my home to help counteract some of the mold and pollen spores that get in the air. Toxins can affect your immune system, leaving you sluggish and decrease your mental awareness. They work their way into muscles, organs and nerve cells causing damage and disease.

When I think of all this, I am glad God created us with wonderful immune systems that fight off the toxins and disease entities that threaten us. He also gave us tips on how to increase and improve our longevity.

Our bodies are always working to expel and eliminate these toxins through the air we exhale, kidney and bowel function and our sweat glands. We can take simple steps to combat the effects of our toxic world. A steamy shower or sauna treatment works wonders as it opens our skins pores to excrete the toxins. Our skin is the largest organ of our bodies and can excrete large of amounts of chemical buildup through our sweat. I enjoy and look forward to a hot steamy shower... I recommend drinking water after this routine to hydrate yourself from the fluid volume you've lost through sweating. Keeping the shower area clean with chemical free cleaners helps reduce buildup of harsh chemicals or molds so the air you're breathing through the steam is fresher and cleaner. We can work up a sweat through exercise, but be cautious if you have health problems. Check with your doctor regarding any new thing you try. Start slowly and in small increments. This was something I've learned on my health journey. We tend to overdo everything. I did this year's ago with an exercise regime and caused a severe back muscle strain.

Many detoxification programs include fasting. Even the Bible informs us that fasting removes toxins from our system and can promote clarity in our thinking and ability to hear from God. There's a lot to be said for fasting. If you're considering a fast read up on it first. The most important thing to remember is anytime you are cleansing your body you must replace the important nutrients that are lost along with the waste.

Vitamins, minerals and enzymes are the important nutrients that feed our body with energy and boost our immune systems. Probiotics contain specific bacteria that aid gastro-intestinal health, and promote an optimal functioning immune system. They keep our digestive tracts blossoming with healthy intestinal bacteria, and overcome the damage caused by antibiotics and additives in our foods. Learn about healthy foods that fuel your body with energy and vitality. We've heard the saying "You are what you eat."

Diabetics need to eat a healthier diet limiting sugar and massive amounts of carbohydrates, it wouldn't hurt any of us to cut back on these and increase our vegetable intake.

Start with a good healthy vitamin/mineral supplement. Recent research has shown most of us are depleted in Vitamin D which is the sunshine vitamin. Even when we're in the sun you don't always get enough. Using sun block decreases the absorption of vitamin D as well. (However, I'm not suggesting you not use it). If you have good insurance coverage and desire to know what you are specifically depleted in your doctor can do a blood test for vitamins and minerals. Seeing a nutritionist is another alternative health care provider that can instruct on a healthy meal plan and nutritional supplementation.

Health food stores are great places to browse and get free information. If money is tight stick with a good multi-vitamin and mineral supplement and drink water.

Due to my sensitivities I have had trouble with my body handling supplements. I start slow and take what I can. I drink plenty of bottled water but don't overdue and I walk regularly.

When shopping for groceries the rule for adding nutritionally sound food to your basket is to shop on the outer perimeters of the store. That way you hit the isles with fresh produce adding fresh fruits and vegetables to your diet. You also find dairy products, poultry, and lean meat on the outer edges of the store. When my friend and I taught childbirth classes we made this recommendation to our clients. My friend was exposed to this teaching when she attended Weight Watchers. It's also a tip for dieters to stay out of the isle with the cookies and foods that contain high sugar content. If sugar isn't a problem for you, I say treat yourself once or twice a week to a sweet treat.

Massage: Massaging muscles removes the toxins lodged within them and helps transport them to the lymph nodes for elimination. In nursing school I was taught some techniques for massaging muscles. You can read some books and learn a few techniques or pamper yourself with a professional message.

Wash Your Hands: In Nursing 101 the first thing we learned was the most important step in germ warfare is good hand washing. It not only protects others from the spread of contagious disease, but protects you as well. Although soap helps, the most important point is scrubbing your hands together for at least 10 seconds. The friction dislodges the dirt and grime.

Sleep and Rest: Some people don't need as much sleep as others, but I recommend getting your beauty rest. God instituted the Sabbath so we could rest, relax and worship. Rest is an important component to our health and beauty. A good night's sleep is essential as it rejuvenates and repairs the cells in our bodies. It keeps us from having bags and dark circles under our eyes. (However, this can also be a symptom of allergies).

Experts recommend sleeping at least 6-8 hours a night. In nursing school I learned babies, children and teens need more sleep than adults. As we age we acquire hormone imbalances and illnesses that can have an effect on our sleep. There are many natural remedies containing sleep hormones such Melatonin on the market. If you're on a medication, check with the Pharmacist before taking one and see that there are no negative interactions with your medication. Otherwise, check with your physician. A glass of warm milk taken before bed is an old-fashioned remedy for sleep. Warming the milk releases the Melatonin the milk contains. Adding a little natural, raw honey to the milk is supposed to aid in sleep as well. A warm bath or shower can help relax you and make you sleepy.

Sleep disorders such as insomnia or lack of ability to sleep can be due to drinking too much caffeine or ingesting it too late into the evening.

My husband and a good friend of mine love to take power naps. They feel refreshed getting at least 20 good minutes of sleep mid-afternoon. Although this isn't always possible, a short time of rest (even relaxing at lunch) can help rejuvenate the mind and help you feel mentally alert. I enjoy taking an afternoon break to sit and daydream. I notice I can feel rested and inspired. Napping too long can pose a problem with your ability to fall asleep when bedtime arrives. Be aware not to nap for too long.

Body Language: I chide that a smile is God's face lift! Because it is a natural wrinkle reducer as it fights a frown which is gravity pulling our facial muscles downward! Wearing a daily frown just makes us produce wrinkles that much faster.

― ～

Accentuate Your Positive.

"Consider how the lilies grow. They do not labor or spin. Yet I tell you, not even Solomon in his entire splendor was dressed like one of these... How much more will God clothe you?"

~LUKE 12:27, 28 (NIV)

Have you ever noticed pharmacies and local department store name sections in the store health and beauty? Even magazines have health and beauty sections for their readers. There is a connection between how we feel and how we look. I understand that many times when we don't feel good we don't feel like keeping up our personal hygiene up, combing our hair or brushing our teeth (I've been there).

When I was housebound I dressed in plain cotton dresses. Eventually they faded, but they felt comfy like those old pair of shoes. Because my sensitivities were great and I was detoxifying my body of chemicals, I didn't wear any make-up or color my hair. (Since I was a teenager in modeling school, I enjoyed wearing make-up and selecting fashionable outfits. I took pleasure in looking good). Each time I looked in the mirror I missed that well-groomed woman I used to be. Then I started researching minerals make-up without the harsh chemicals. Just a touch of blush lit my face up again! (A word of caution, if anyone is challenged with sensitivities like me, take note, I had to try several minerals make-ups because my body couldn't handle a load of minerals that were too powerful).

Have you ever noticed when you're feeling sick, depressed or ugly when you look in the mirror you feel worse? If you do just a little something and look in the mirror it brightens your outlook. It did for me.

I heard a story of a woman who had her lip bit off from a dog. She would go to the mirror and speak positive words to herself about how good her lip looked. This didn't make sense, but as she believed she reproduced. Eventually her lip grew back!

When we shower we feel refreshed. When we are well-groomed (this tip goes for men too. I'm always encouraging my sons to look their best), we feel better, and this is proven to help our self-esteem. Just knowing we look better on the outside can make us feel better on the inside.

Sometimes, we get out of balance, thinking God wants us to look drab or dowdy. Somehow, we think holiness means being plain. God is all about color and splendor. When He designed the priestly garments he included twelve dazzling gemstones to be placed across the front of the breastplates. I have a blouse that has some clear stones at the neckline. Each time I wear it someone compliments on how it lights up my face.

Due to age, income, low energy or poor self-worth we, oftentimes, put on a few extra pounds; we get comfortable with our lives thinking it doesn't matter how we look anyway. I think a few sparkling earrings, a top which hides a few flaws, or a colorful shirt can lift our spirits and the souls of those around us. Who knows that some marriages might be saved if the spouse decided to add a touch of class to their appearance?

Even on a tight budget you can dress your best. I met one of my closest friends in nursing school. I admired how nice she always looked. Her clothes matched and she wore a scarf to accessorize her outfit and add a touch of color. One day I complimented her on her wardrobe. She told me her secret was buying her clothes at resale shops. With a family and school tuition she couldn't afford to shop at boutiques or department stores.

Hand-me-downs can work as well. The first outfit I wore to speak at a church event was hand-me-downs from my sister. My budget was tight and I hadn't shopped in years. My sister gave me a beautiful blue sweater with a few clear gemstones on it. The light blue jean skirt she offered me was a great match. My friend gave me a pair of dark blue tights and I wore some black shoes my niece passed on to me. I'll never forget how good I looked that day. I was amazed when I was in the restroom washing my hands and a perfect stranger shared how much she liked my outfit. Even though I still wasn't feeling my best physically, doing my best to look good helped me feel good. I still struggle with that each day.

Don't forget to embrace your body style. There are many fashionable items for full figures these days; don't allow any excuse to stop you from looking your best. With some ingenuity and creativity you can find a way. I believe when we look good on the outside we feel good on the inside. My mother, as well as my modeling school instructor, always cautioned me to stand tall. Because I was taller than most girls my age I tended to slouch. I discovered keeping my shoulders back and my head high made me feel more confident. Good body posture promotes excellent muscular skeletal health; it facilitates proper flow of energy through nerves, keeps bones in alignment and allows the blood to flow adequately through our veins.

Remember the best part of our beauty (the part God delights in), is our inner life. When I went to modeling school the class I enjoyed the most was Social Graces. I like to say social grace is extending God's grace. It's how we treat others. That's what is beautiful in God's sight. We need to make it a point to study our Bible and learn the ways we are to treat others. That's the true display of health and beauty! We can all be beautiful.

With your health and beauty in order, you're on your way to your dream. But make sure you read the next chapter; there's one more powerful and important step.

Here are some affirmations I speak over my life for health and wholeness. You can enjoy them too!

I dwell in Your secret place of the Most High and rest in Your shadow Almighty, I say, You are my refuge, my God, in whom I trust. You will save me from the deadly pestilence. A thousand may fall at my side, ten thousand at my right hand, but it will not come near me. You will command Your angels charge over me to protect and defend me. You will deliver me and honor me and with long life satisfy me (see Psalm 91).

Lord, You send Your Word and heal me and rescue me from the pit and destruction (see Psalm 107:20).

Your Words are health to my body and healing to my flesh (Proverbs 4:22).

God has not given me a spirit of fear, but power, love and a sound mind (1 Timothy 1:17).

I prosper and am in health, even as my soul prospers (see 3 John 2).

My healing, restoration and the power of a new life springs forth speedily (see Isaiah 58:8).

God is restoring my health and healing my wounds (see Jeremiah 30:17).

Long life to me, good health to me and my household (Samuel 25:6).

I believe you Love me, Lord, and I receive Your love, because Love heals.

15

Pray and Praise-The MIRACLE Working Power to Bring Forth Your Dreams

"Lord, teach us to pray."

~ LUKE 11:1

It's comforting that heaven listens and sends mysterious answers to our prayers. It's an amazing concept that God hears our praise and prayers and brings miraculous answers. Sometimes the miracles come as wise practical solutions to our problems. Other times, they are amazing things that happen and are without explanation-other than a God occurrence- of how they could have happened!

When I have a great need, I am encouraged knowing God cares and listens to my prayers. Everything written in this book is an answer to my prayers and the guidance I have received due to them.

I have so many amazing stories regarding answered prayers recorded in my journal. One of my favorites is about my small plaster plaque that says, "Prayer changes Things." It sits on the shelf by my family photos. One day while washing dishes I heard a loud crash. I ran in the living to see what happened. The boys had been roughhousing and all my photos were knocked from the top of the entertainment center. There was glass everywhere. Glancing down, my heart sunk, when I noticed my precious plaque was broken. I recall the gut wrenching feeling in the pit of my stomach as I observed small splinters of plaster, broken glass and twisted picture frames scattered all over the living room floor. Over time, I was able to replace some of the broken picture frames with new ones, but my plaque was irreplaceable. I searched Christian bookstores and specialty shops all over the county and beyond, but never found a replacement. Several years later at my wedding shower I lifted the lid on a small gift box and unraveled the tissue paper surrounding the gift to reveal a plaque identical to the one I lost. The mystery is that the person who gave it to me knew nothing about my plaque! There was truly a powerful message in those three words, "Prayer Changes Things."

There are many reasons we pray. The greatest reason is to communicate with God. As human beings we were created to relate and communicate. I enjoy the example that as we converse with our children, God enjoys conversing with His children, in the same way. Prayer is a way we can connect with God and fulfill His plans and dreams for our lives as we ask His direction and we learn to listen to His voice.

As a young girl there were times I was too timid and shy to approach my father with a want or need, so I held back. Eventually, I learned I didn't have to be afraid of my dad. He loved me and encouraged me to express my needs. Sometimes, we feel too timid and shy to ask God for anything. We hold back our true feelings and emotions. We forget God knows more about us than we do and He understands our feelings, besides. The beauty of our relationship with Him is that we don't need to be timid and shy or hold anything from Him. We're informed to come boldly to His throne! (Hebrews 4:16). Prayers should be clearly expressed from the heart, personal and specific to our dreams and desires as we make our requests known to God. Like a child becoming comfortable with a parent, communicating with our Lord is something we develop and become relaxed doing.

I recall as a young girl kneeling at my bedside, my mother at my side, learning to say a simple bedtime prayer. Over the years, I stretched my ability to pray throughout the day. It's something we should do before beginning any activity. It shields us with protection and comforts our emotions. It provides us with the power and wisdom to accomplish God's purpose in trying situations. As we spend time throughout the day communicating with our heavenly Father helps us become more intimate with Him, (as previously mentioned in chapter one), and provides the strength and direction we need to make it through our day.

When our prayers are coming from our heads and not our hearts, they can feel unexciting and unmoving. This can happen when they are just read off the page or we repeat the same phrases over and over again, with no real meaning or passion behind what we are doing or saying. However, to help us we can pray from a book or a church bulletin, as long as the prayers come from our hearts.

James 5:16 says, "The earnest (heartfelt, continued) prayer of a righteous man makes tremendous power available (dynamic in its working)."

I love this passage. It reveals the prayer straight from our hearts have the same power as dynamite! Dynamite gets its root from the word dynamic.

At times when we're frustrated or afraid and we're not sure what to pray for or how to ask, we can ask like the disciples did, *"Lord, teach us to pray."*

I enjoy prayer because it feels good to know my needs have been voiced to God and He is working on my behalf.

Prayer is so unique to each situation. It requires no special posture, and can be expressed in our own way. Jesus prayed many ways, he held his hands raised up in the air, or the typical way with fingers folded together, other times, He prayed with His hands opened wide toward heaven. He also prayed while standing, sitting, kneeling, or laying on his face to the ground.

I pray many ways and in a variety of places- even while doing dishes or running an errand. God goes with us everywhere and we need His help to guide us every step of the way. We can even pray silently during a conversation when we need the wisdom to know what to say.

There are special types of prayer: Some Christians pray in a miraculous heavenly language given to them known as tongues. This is explained in Bible passages in 1Corinthians chapter 14. However, don't be apprehensive over this, God hears our simple prayers as well. Remember, I started praying as a child when my mother taught me the simple bedtime prayer, "Now I lay me down to sleep." You can't get simpler than childlike faith.

As a nurse praying for physical healing for my patients was something I did on a daily basis. Besides beseeching on behalf of my patients, I had other opportunities to pray for friends, family members, and my own life issues. Jesus gave us many examples of this type of prayer.

When we are distressed over financial issues, we can pray for help with our finances. Prayer covers any type of personal need we have. We can even ask for emotional stability. Scripture informs us in the book of Psalms that God knows the number of hairs on our head. That's why we can get personal with Him.

Fasting and prayer is another spiritual discipline mature Christians take part in. The particulars are between you and God. People fast various things. Some refrain from watching T.V., withhold spending on a certain item, or refrain from food for a particular time frame. There are many wonderful books written on the spiritual discipline of fasting and prayer.

A prayer of praise and thanksgiving is an important piece of prayer that shows we appreciate God and the things He does for us. There is power in our praise. A praise could consist of a shout, an acknowledging word such as, praise God! Hallelujah (which means praise be to God), is also often used in praise. The raising of hands extended in thanksgiving is another form of praise. Sing a song to the Lord is a special way we praise the Lord and is how most church services begin.

You can pray for God's grace when you need strength. You can ask for favor to help you with people in your life such as a spouse, boss or other. You can request favor from God to help you obtain a job or to be successful at what you do. The prayer of Jabez is popular prayer taken from Scripture that models a prayer for favor.

You can pray this same prayer. . .

"Oh, that You would bless me, and enlarge my border, and that Your hand might be with me, and You would keep me from evil so it might not hurt me! And God granted his request." (1 Chronicles 4:10).

When something good happens to my husband he exclaims, "I got the FOG today!" meaning the favor of God.

When we ask God to enlarge our territory we are essentially asking God to help us make a bigger impact for Him. Whatever our purpose is we want it to impact and bless many! Whether in our business, ministry, family or owning property this prayer applies receiving better opportunities and BIG dreams.

Prayer and praise opens the windows of heaven and closes the gates of hell from prevailing against us.

God desires us to have big dreams, daring prayers, and receive BIG results so we can make a big impact on the world in which we live!

As a nurse I enjoy learning scientific facts. A major university conducted a scientific study on prayer. They took two groups of patient's recovering from heart surgery. The group prayed for had either none or fewer complications than the group not prayed for. Another study that was conducted with two Petri dishes. Each of them were contaminated with bacteria. Only one of the dishes was prayed over. The dish prayed over had no growth or very slow growth. The other had abundant amounts of bacteria.

When we pray we invite the supernatural to partner with us. When your dream wants to fade away and the devil is taunting you, "you'll never achieve it," believe in the power of prayer and do what the Bible says, "resist the devil at his onset." Use prayer and praise God and don't allow the devil to distract you from your God-given assignment.

While housebound, prayer was the vehicle that helped me discover BIG dreams! It's my desire to help you, precious reader, to dream bigger than ever and receive a prosperous life. I hope I have helped you with some of the simple principles in this book.

Here's a prayer of faith to help you be born again (a Spiritual birth) and receive eternal life through Jesus Christ sacrificial death on the cross.

Father God, I thank you for sacrificing Your Son, Jesus Christ, Who, died in my place and rose again, so I can be forgiven of my sins. Please forgive me. I choose to make Jesus my Savior and Lord. Thank you for making my dream to live eternally in heaven with you a reality. Fill me with your Holy Spirit and fulfill your dream and purpose for my life on earth, In Jesus name, Amen.

May you keep dreaming BIG and impossible dreams! And use the steps presented in this book to help you realize them!

Closing Sentiments

Congratulations, readers! You've made it through the steps to help you fulfill your dreams. I hope you have experienced some powerful, transforming changes while reading through them. But, remember, every day for the rest of your life these will be important steps to put into practice. If you need a gentle reminder of the steps, just view the contents page at the beginning of the book.

It is my prayer that you continue to grow and reach your potential. Drop me a line and let me know how you are doing on your dream steps!

Blessings and Love,
Annettee

About the Author

Annettee Budzban is a Christian Author, Inspirational Speaker, Registered Nurse and Motivational Life Coach who coaches groups or one-to-one sessions. She is also a devoted wife, mother and grandmother who resides in the Chicagoland area.

Since childhood, Annettee, has embraced a special love for Jesus Christ and the Spiritual principles found in the Bible. She enjoys teaching the Word of God intertwined with examples and applications for practical daily life.

Her passion for birthing led her to a 17 year career as an Entrepreneur Nurse Childbirth Educator. She also enjoyed her active 18 year career as a nurse manager. Her clinical nursing experience includes areas of pediatrics, O.B. mental health and family practice. Later in her nursing career she was the nurse spokesperson for a T.V. advertisement for Cancer Treatment Centers of America and the keynote speaker at their conference held for nationwide volunteers.

Annettee's career took a turn of events when she was struck with an illness that left her housebound for eight years. During this time, she had to give up her dreams. She suffered grief and sorrow over the loss of an active life and career. It was during this time that her strong faith in the Lord and motivated spirit helped her overcome adversity, brought her a new purpose and direction and expanded her dreams.

In her process of recovery, she graces a variety of audiences with joy and hope for healing their mind, body and spirit as she shares how God helped her though her life struggles, which include: health, financial and relational challenges. She successfully navigated her way as a single divorced mother for ten years, and then her personal health struggles, (being housebound for eight years). She expresses God's miracle working power and great ability to help others to live with passion, discover and fulfill their purpose, and birth BIG dreams in the midst of trials and adversity.

Her writings have appeared over 1,000 times in print publications such as *Guideposts Magazine*, and *Guideposts Books*, New York Times Best Seller, *Chicken Soup for the Recovering Soul, Nursing Spectrum, Psychology for Living* and various other Christian publications. Her newspaper column *Inspirations* is featured weekly in several newspapers.

Books and CDs

You can contact Annettee Budzban to purchase an autographed book or CD

Books

Life Changing Inspirations

Spend a Moment with God

When Heaven Whispers

Inspirations to Restore Your Soul

CD's

Dream Big! Make Your Dream Reality

Inspirations for a Better Life

Write and Publish for Fun and Profit

Contact Information

E-mail   Annetteebudzban@aol.com

Phone   224-637-9438

Website   www.Annetteebudzban.com

P.O. box 532 Grayslake, Il. 60030

Other books include

Chicken Soup for the Recovering Soul: Daily Inspirations

Chicken Soup for the Soul: Inspiration for Nurses

Guideposts Miracles of Nature

Guideposts Extraordinary Answers to Prayer from Tragedy to Triumph

Newspaper Column Inspirations

Daily Herald Lake County, IL

Zion-Benton News

Annettee Coaches

As a Life Coach I will encourage you to live the most fulfilling life you can. I will pray for you and help you formulate goals that will help you reach your full potential.

In my gentle approach I will listen to your heart's desire, give God centered advice, and treat you with respect.

My Coaching is for you if you need:

To grow spiritually.

To develop and reach your potential.

To discover God-given gifts or purpose.

To grow in confidence or overcome shyness.

To start your career in writing or speaking.

To overcome a loss or make a transition in life.

Start your journey to succeed at living your best life, now. Contact me Annettee Budzban by e-mail at Annetteebudzban@aol.com, or by calling or txt at 224-637-9438 for a life coaching session or to speak at your conference or retreat. I'm also available for those breakfast, luncheon, or group meetings. We can discuss a fee to fit your budget!

Relax, you don't have to live in my neighborhood, I can coach by phone or Skype. It's the newest technique in coaching and counseling!

Disclaimer

In writing this book it is my desire to see you achieve your dream. However, the results are up to you. I can't make any guarantees. But these are principles, strategies, and methods from the Bible that have proved helpful to me. I pray you find them helpful as well, as you discover and implement them to move toward the fulfillment of your dream.

81756713R00086

Made in the USA
Lexington, KY
21 February 2018